CONTENTS

Foreword v

Acknowledgments vii

How to Use This Course xi

Twelfth Night or What You Will 1

    Introduction to the Play 1
    Lesson Assignments 3
    Learning Objectives 3
    Synopsis of the Play 4
    " 'Are You Mad? Or What Are You?': Revelry and Revelation in *Twelfth Night*" by Gayle Greene 6
    Annotated Bibliography 16
    Self-test 18

The Tragedy of King Richard the Second 21

    Introduction to the Play 21
    Lesson Assignments 25
    Learning Objectives 25
    Synopsis of the Play 26
    "*Richard II*: An Experiment in Staging" by Michael Mullin 28
    Annotated Bibliography 51
    Self-test 53

The First Part of King Henry the Fourth 59

    Introduction to the Play 59
    Lesson Assignments 62
    Learning Objectives 62
    Synopsis of the Play 63
    "The Trials of King and Prince: *The First Part of King Henry the Fourth*" by Jay L. Halio 65
    Annotated Bibliography 77
    Self-test 79

The Second Part of King Henry the Fourth   83

   Introduction to the Play   83
   Lesson Assignments   86
   Learning Objectives   86
   Synopsis of the Play   87
   "*Henry IV, Part Two* and the Aesthetics of Failure" by Stephen Booth   89
   Annotated Bibliography   101
   Self-test   103

The Life of King Henry the Fifth   107

   Introduction to the Play   107
   Lesson Assignments   110
   Learning Objectives   110
   Synopsis of the Play   111
   "Seeing *Henry V* 'Perspectively' " by Philip C. McGuire   115
   Annotated Bibliography   128
   Self-test   130

The Tempest   135

   Introduction to the Play   135
   Lesson Assignments   137
   Learning Objectives   137
   Synopsis of the Play   138
   "*The Tempest*: Parallels and Parodies" by Joan Hartwig   140
   Annotated Bibliography   149
   Self-test   151

THE SHAKESPEARE PLAYS

A Study Guide for the Second Season

developed by
**University Extension
University of California, San Diego**
and
The Coast Community Colleges

Development of educational materials for The Shakespeare Plays is funded jointly by grants from the Corporation for Public Broadcasting and from the underwriters of the television series broadcast by the Public Broadcasting Service: Exxon Corporation, Morgan Guaranty Trust, and Metropolitan Life Insurance Company.

KENDALL/HUNT PUBLISHING COMPANY
2460 Kerper Boulevard,
Dubuque, Iowa 52001

University of California, San Diego

Martin N. Chamberlain
Dean for Academic Affairs
University Extension

Mary Lindenstein Walshok
Associate Dean for Academic Affairs
University Extension

Kiki Skagen Munshi
Program Development Coordinator
University Extension

The Coast Community Colleges

Norman E. Watson
Chancellor
The Coast Community Colleges

Bernard J. Luskin
President
Coastline Community College

Thomas H. Gripp
Dean of Telecourse Development

Michael V. Olds
Instructional Designer

Louise Matthews Hewitt
Telecourse Editor

Valerie Lynch Lee
Study Guide Editor

David P. Stone
Test Bank Developer

Carl Glassford
Illustrator

Excerpt from *Richard II*, Act IV, scene i, lines 107–200, is from William Shakespeare, *Richard II*, edited by Matthew W. Black, in The Pelican Shakespeare, General Editor: Alfred Harbage. Rev. ed. New York: Penguin Books, 1970. Copyright © Penguin Books, Inc., 1957, 1970. Reprinted by permission of Penguin Books.

Copyright © 1980 by The Regents of the University of California and the Coast Community College District.

Library of Congress Catalog Card Number: 79-91452

ISBN 0-8403-2149-X

All rights reserved. No part of this publication may be reproduced, stored in a retrieval system, or transmitted, in any form or by any means electronic, mechanical, photocopying, recording, or otherwise, without the prior written permission of the copyright owner.

Printed in the United States of America

B   402149   01

FOREWORD

Welcome to the second season of THE SHAKESPEARE PLAYS. As in season one, the British Broadcasting Corporation, in association with Time-Life Television, has offered us five new television productions of the dramatic works of William Shakespeare plus a rebroadcast of *Richard II* from season one. And as in season one, the Corporation for Public Broadcasting has joined with the American underwriters for the series—Exxon Corporation, Metropolitan Life Insurance Company and Morgan Guaranty Trust Company of New York—to sponsor the development of educational materials and activities in support of the series.

Most of these materials and activities are specifically keyed to particular audiences. For example, TelEd, Inc. of Los Angeles is producing posters, long-playing records, teachers' guides, and ditto-masters for use in secondary schools. WNET/Thirteen in New York City, the producing station for THE SHAKESPEARE PLAYS, is preparing a handsome 32-page Viewers' Guide for use in our homes. And National Public Radio, which offered a variety of special programs on Shakespeare during season one, is producing new background offerings for broadcast in year two—programs that will appeal primarily to mature adult listeners.

Like the other materials and activities currently being developed, this study guide is designed primarily for the needs of an identifiable audience: the students in this country who attend two- or four-year community colleges, colleges, and universities. It is intended to be used as part of a formal course offering that focuses on Shakespeare televised. For that reason, it has been devised and produced by two institutions with distinguished records in the formulation and dissemination of college-level telecourses: the University of California San Diego and The Coast Community Colleges. Under the supervision of an Educational Advisory Panel for THE SHAKESPEARE PLAYS, extension division of UCSD and the design staff of Coastline Community College, one of The Coast Community Colleges, commissioned essays and other ancillary activities from leading teachers of Shakespeare, and negotiated arrangements for distribution of the materials produced.

The results, I trust, will fully justify the time and expense invested. As in season one, I am sure that formal telecourses on THE SHAKESPEARE PLAYS will prove popular and valuable, enhancing the viewing and reading experience of those students who take advantage of this unusual opportunity to encounter the works of the greatest dramatist and poet the world has ever known.

At the same time, however, it would please me—and it would please the producers and sponsors of this study guide—if others found these materials of interest. I think, for example, of informal Shakespeare study groups, of community library discussion circles, of groups of high-school English teachers who might wish to read, see, and explore THE SHAKESPEARE PLAYS together. For it is a mistake to think that Shakespeare is meant to be appreciated and studied only in formal classroom settings. When his works were first published in a collected edition—the First Folio of 1623—the compilers and editors of that volume addressed their preface "To the great Variety of Readers." Let us hope that one of the benefits of THE SHAKESPEARE PLAYS—and of such supporting materials as this study guide—will be to broaden Shakespeare's audience once again, to make his life and work accessible to as many readers and viewers as possible. After all, as Ben Jonson noted in his commendatory verses in the First Folio, Shakespeare "was not of an age, but for all time"—a playwright who remains alive today, as important to our own cultural life in the twentieth century as he was to the golden age of the English Renaissance.

John F. Andrews
Director of Academic Programs
Folger Shakespeare Library

ACKNOWLEDGMENTS

The development of the educational materials for each play in this telecourse was supervised by an outstanding scholar and teacher in Shakespeare studies. Each also contributed an original essay to the materials on his or her play.

Stephen Booth, Ph.D., professor of English at the University of California, Berkeley, contributed materials for *2 Henry IV*. He was educated at Harvard and Trinity College, Cambridge, England. His published works include *The Book Called Holinshed's Chronicles, An Essay on Shakespeare's Sonnets,* and, most recently, *An Annotated Edition of Shakespeare's Sonnets,* for which he won the James Russell Lowell Prize. Booth's essays on Shakespeare's plays have appeared in numerous anthologies, and his articles on Shakespeare have been published in such periodicals as *Shakespeare Quarterly, Modern Language Quarterly,* and *The New York Review of Books.* He has a book entitled *King Lear, Macbeth, Definition and Tragedy* in progress.

Gayle Greene, Ph.D., who contributed materials on *Twelfth Night* to this study guide, received her education from the University of California, Berkeley, and Columbia University. At present, she is an assistant professor of English at Scripps College, Claremont, California. She is the author of numerous articles on Shakespeare, which have appeared or will soon appear in such periodicals as *Journal of Women's Studies in Literature, Studia Neophilologica, Renaissance Drama,* and *Studies in English Literature.* She has coedited a book, *The Woman's Part: Feminist Criticism of Shakespeare,* and is currently working on another book, the subject of which is linguistic skepticism in Shakespeare's plays.

Joan Hartwig, Ph.D., is associate professor of English at the University of Kentucky. She was educated at Northwestern University, the University of Florida, Gainesville, and Washington University, St. Louis. Her *Shakespeare's Tragicomic Vision* was published by Louisiana State University Press. Hartwig's articles have appeared in *College English, Yearbook of English Studies, Renaissance Papers,* and numerous other journals. In addition, she has twice been published in the *Journal of English Literary History* and has contributed reviews to *Shakespeare Studies,* and the *Shakespeare Quarterly.* She is currently working on a book tentatively titled "Shakespeare's Puzzling Analogical Scenes." She contributed material on *The Tempest* to this study guide.

Jay L. Halio, Ph.D., contributor of material on *1 Henry IV*, is professor of English and associate provost for instruction at the University of Delaware. He received his undergraduate degree at Syracuse University and his graduate degrees at Yale University. His professional associations include the Modern Language Association, the Renaissance Society of America, the Renaissance Conference (Middle Atlantic States), and the Shakespeare Association of America. In addition, he has served on the Board of Directors of the World Centre for Shakespeare Studies and is presently on the Central Executive Committee of the Folger Institute of Renaissance Studies. Halio has written or edited seven books, including casebooks of essays on Shakespeare's plays and old spelling editions of the plays. Among the periodicals in which his scholarly and critical articles on Shakespeare and Elizabethan literature have appeared are *Modern Language Notes, College English, Studies in English Literature, Shakespeare Quarterly*, and *Shakespeare Studies*. His works in progress include "Nightingales That Roar: The Dramatic Language of *Midsummer Night's Dream*," and "Dramatic Action in *King John*."

Philip C. McGuire, Ph.D., associate professor of English, provided the materials on *Henry V* for this study guide. He received his bachelor's degree from LaSalle College and master's and doctorate from Stanford University. He was the recipient of a Folger Shakespeare Library Research Fellowship in 1970 and has served as a visiting lecturer in English at the University of Lancaster in England. He has coedited one book, *Shakespeare: The Theatrical Dimension*, which included one of his essays: "Choreography and Language in *Richard II*." McGuire's articles have appeared in many journals, including *The Times Higher Education Supplement, Shakespeare Quarterly*, and *Studies in English Literature*. He has also presented his professional papers to such organizations as the Central Conference of the Renaissance Society of America, the Modern Language Association, and the Shakespeare Association of America. McGuire is currently working on a book entitled, *"Language in Their Very Gesture": Shakespeare's Plays and the Limits of Literary Study*.

Michael Mullin, Ph.D., the contributor of materials on *Richard II*, is associate professor of English at the University of Illinois, Urbana. He was educated at Holy Cross College, Worcester, Massachusetts, and Yale University, has held an observership with the Royal Shakespeare Company, Stratford-on-Avon, and was an Interdisciplinary Fellow in Theatre at the University of Illinois. He is the founder and director of the Shakespeare Film COOP and served on the corporation for Public Broadcasting's National Advisory Committee for THE SHAKESPEARE PLAYS on television. He has a large number of publications to his credit, including *Macbeth Onstage,* and is now working on a book about *Antony and Cleopatra.*

The Shakespeare Plays Educational Advisory Panel was instrumental in providing overall guidance and support for the educational programs connected with THE SHAKESPEARE PLAYS. The committee included:

Chairman:
John F. Andrews, editor, the *Shakespeare Quarterly,* Folger Shakespeare Library, Washington, D.C.

Members:
Elizabeth A. Barnes, teacher of speech and drama, Bowie High School, Bowie, Maryland, representing the Secondary School Theatre Association.

David S. Rodes, professor of English, University of California, Los Angeles.

Gladys Veidemanis, chairman, English Department, North High School, Oshkosh, Wisconsin, representing the National Council of Teachers of English.

HOW TO USE THIS COURSE

If the title *The Shakespeare Plays: A Study Guide for the Second Season* sounds suspiciously like "How to See Europe on Ten Dollars a Day," there's a good reason. This book is intended to serve as your tour guide through the six plays selected for this course. Regardless of which edition of Shakespeare's plays you intend to use in this course, this guide should serve as your basic reference. It suggests how to prepare to watch each televised play, what to look for in that play, and what to expect from each experience. It also provides you with tests.

The basic aim of this television series, THE SHAKESPEARE PLAYS, is to enable you to experience a play with understanding and appreciation. More specifically, it is hoped that, by the end of this course, you will also be able to:

1. Cite examples of the ways in which Shakespeare's text is a script that gives clues for performance.
2. Identify major characters, discuss the problems they face, and show how they deal with them.
3. Describe the various groups of characters and discuss their interaction.
4. Identify the main locales of action and explain their significance.
5. Trace the sequence of events and suggest why the scenes are ordered as they are.
6. Identify differences in the ways the various characters speak, and show how language—metaphor, diction, verse and prose forms, jokes, wordplay, and the like—contribute to the interest and meaning of the play.
7. Explore the relationship between the printed text and the televised performances.
8. Discuss the various possible interpretations of scenes, characters, and entire themes that are supported by the evidence of the text.
9. Relate the major themes of the various plays to human experience.

The principal components of this telecourse include the televised plays, the texts of the plays, and the study guide.

THE TELEVISED PLAYS

The six plays by William Shakespeare are *Twelfth Night, Richard II, 1 Henry IV, 2 Henry IV, Henry V,* and *The Tempest.* These plays have been especially selected for this second season of the series, known collectively as THE SHAKESPEARE PLAYS, which is being coproduced by the British Broadcasting Corporation and Time-Life Television and aired in the United States over the more than 250 stations of the Public Broadcasting Service. The ambitious plan of THE SHAKESPEARE PLAYS project is to produce all thirty-seven dramas by Shakespeare for television over a period of six years.

The productions are neither photographed stage plays nor movies. These are *television* performances that exploit camera angles, closeups, reaction shots, detailed sets, cutaways, background music, location and studio shooting, and various other television techniques that clarify and heighten meaning and emotion. In this way, each television production is a distinct interpretation of a Shakespeare play.

THE TEXTS OF THE PLAYS

A single edition of the plays has not been designated for this telecourse. There are simply too many good editions of Shakespeare on the market for the course designers to select a single one for use with this course. The institutions offering this course or the instructors of record may decide to make such a recommendation, or you may select from among a number of very acceptable versions of Shakespeare's works—either complete editions or individual plays—depending on your particular needs, inclinations, and budget.

For the sake of uniformity and to have a common point of reference, however, all quotations from the seven plays and all citations (by act, scene, and line) mentioned in the essays and other materials in this study guide are based on *The Pelican Shakespeare* edition, published by Viking/Penguin, Inc. The BBC, however, uses *The Alexander Text of the Complete Works of William Shakespeare,* published by William Collins Sons and Company, Ltd., as the basis for its television productions. The Pelican Shakespeare edition was selected because it represents the latest in modern scholarship, contains helpful introductory materials, includes a handy glossary of Elizabethan terms, and is widely available in bookstores throughout the United States.

Be prepared, therefore, for minor textual discrepancies and line references if you are using another edition or if you elect to follow a script other than The Alexander Text as you watch the televised plays. In most cases, act and scene references will be identical in all editions—television will not pause for scene changes—but line references may vary slightly, particularly in prose passages (as opposed to poetry). Remember, too, that the directors of the televised plays have also edited Shakespeare's script to meet their own technical and artistic requirements; consequently, you may have to hunt around a bit to find the exact words of a particular speech, but, with a little diligence and perseverance, these should be quickly found.

THE STUDY GUIDE

The study guide is a key component of this telecourse because it integrates the print materials with the television productions and makes the whole course comprehensible. The study guide has one lesson for each of the seven plays of the telecourse, and each lesson is composed of seven parts: Introduction to the Play, Lesson Assignments, Learning Objectives, Synopsis of the Play, an original essay, Annotated Bibliography, and Self-test.

The introduction to the Play provides some background about the play itself, offers helpful suggestions about approaching the play, and provides a brief overview of the essay about the play.

The introduction is followed by Lesson Assignments: specific instructions about the sequence in which you should read the text of the play, view the television production, read the essay about the play, and take the Self-test. The sequence of assignments for each play was specially developed by the author of the essay for that play and varies from play to play. The sequence suggested by the author is designed to enhance your insight and appreciation of each play's unique qualities, so it is particularly important to follow the sequence carefully. You may, for example, be asked to read the entire text of the play first, even before reading the essay. You may be asked to focus on a particular sequence of scenes. Or you may be asked to move back and forth between essay and text. Do not simply assume that you can watch the television production "cold" and catch up later on the work outlined in the study guide. Chances are you will be unprepared for the experience and miss a valuable opportunity to explore the many facets of each play that most casual audiences never experience. Resolve at the outset of this course to place yourself in the capable hands of our Shakespearean experts, then follow their directions.

Each lesson also lists Learning Objectives for the entire unit of study designed around the play. These objectives are the learning and performance goals you will be expected to achieve, and will serve as your measure of achievement. These objectives are tailored to the particular play being studied and are quite different from lesson to lesson.

The Learning Objectives are followed by a Synopsis of the Play, or plot summary, which provides you with an overview of what happens in the play. Be sure to read the synopsis at the point directed by the Lesson Assignments.

The essay about the play, written by one of the seven outstanding Shakespearean scholars and teachers who contributed to this study guide, follows the synopsis. Once again, read the essay at the point directed to by the Lesson Assignments.

An Annotated Bibliography has been included after each essay. Each bibliography, compiled by the author of the essay, lists various journal articles, essays, and books to help you in exploring the richness of the play in greater depth and detail.

Finally, each lesson closes with a Self-test that includes multiple-choice questions, short-answer essay questions, and questions for reflection. An Answer Key is supplied for the multiple-choice and short-answer essay questions and provides you with instant feedback that allows you to see what you have accomplished through your study of the play.

The Self-tests have been especially prepared for this course and are designed to test your comprehension and appreciation of THE SHAKESPEARE PLAYS at a number of levels, ranging from a very basic understanding of plot and character to the ability to discuss in considerable depth some of the issues and problems that have engaged Shakespearean scholars in lively debate for centuries. All examination materials are based on the specific learning objectives stated at the beginning of the study unit for each play and on the general course objectives listed in the beginning of this introduction.

The multiple-choice questions deal with the basic elements and concepts in each play. The short-answer essay questions delve more deeply into the subject matter and its treatment by the playwright and require some active thought and concise expression on your part. The questions for reflection require you to consider many of the elements you have studied in the play and integrate them into an opinion that has some substance and documentation. In many instances, these "think" questions are of the type Shakespearean scholars have been debating for centuries. In most cases, there are no definitive answers, nor are you expected to succeed in providing such answers where lifelong students of Shakespeare have failed. You are, however, expected to make an informed effort at an answer, and you may discover to your surprise that you understand more about the play than you may originally have thought. Check with your instructor of record in the course to determine the type of tests for which you will be held responsible.

Finally, just as each play is unique, so is each lesson. Just as you will find that you like some plays better than others, you will find that you like some study techniques better than others. This is natural and to be expected. It is the express purpose of this study guide to introduce you to different approaches and teaching strategies for the study of Shakespeare with the long-range hope that some of these may help you to appreciate and enjoy the richness of Shakespeare's drama, not just in future television productions, but also in the many different stage presentations. If, after taking this course, you find yourself wanting to see other Shakespeare plays in performance, then all of the individuals involved in this telecourse project will consider that their efforts have been most worthwhile.

A SPECIAL NOTE TO THE STUDENT

This course offers you a special opportunity to explore a variety of approaches to Shakespeare's plays. You will read Shakespeare's texts and you will see television's production of the plays. In addition, this guide provides essays by teacher-scholars focusing on different aspects of each play. At some point, the scholars, the actors, and the directors disagree on their interpretations of how a scene should be performed, a character portrayed, or even a single line conveyed. For example, does the jester, Feste, in the television production of *Twelfth Night* prove to be the "shrewdest" character, as Gayle Greene suggests in her essay? Or, to take another example, there may be less movement and gesture in the television production of *Richard II* than Michael Mullin's essay encourages you to imagine in the theater of the mind. Or, to cite a final example, do you find *2 Henry IV* as "disturbingly unpleasant" as Stephen Booth warns? The differing views of these scholars and artists should be understood and respected. Yet throughout this course you should be alert to other possibilities for emphasis and interpretation of what is going on and what it means. To do so is to enjoy and understand Shakespeare's plays.

TWELFTH NIGHT
OR
WHAT YOU WILL

INTRODUCTION TO THE PLAY

Shakespeare cleverly gave this play two titles: *Twelfth Night,* to commemorate the play's first performance on January 6 [1601 or 1602], the twelfth night of Christmas and a particularly festive occasion on the Elizabethan calendar; and *What You Will,* to indicate that there is, in the structure of the play and its characters, something for everyone to enjoy. And, indeed, the play has a bit of everything: a few nimble-witted and resourceful women, a melancholic duke, a majestic and aloof countess, a practical joker named Sir Toby Belch, a comical knight duped out of his money by the practical joker, a puritanical and ambitious steward overreaching himself, a variety of love episodes, a betrayal, a farcical duel between reluctant antagonists, songs of exquisite romance and bawdy exuberance, separated brother-sister twins, a crucial letter that strays into the right/wrong hands, and a woman disguised as a man who unwittingly becomes the object of another woman's love. And all of these characters and events are framed by an idyllic and luxuriant setting: the mythical country of Illyria.

One problem any first-time reader of this play may have is keeping track of the names of the characters. First, many of the names are Italianate—Antonio, Orsino, Cesario, Curio, Maria, Fabian, Sebastian, and Valentine; second, a number of them are almost anagrammatical. For example, the names Olivia, Viola, and Malvolio all contain the same five letters in slightly varied combinations. The confusion of names is compounded by the fact that most of these characters fall into and out of love with each other during the course of the play's action and, to make matters worse, two of these names belong to the same person (Viola/Cesario) who moves into and out of disguise. The reader might be well-advised to make a list of the characters in this play and to jot beside each name some appropriate identifying characteristics, or to devise some other suitable means of remembering who is who. For those who may despair of the task, remember that the difficulty was further compounded in Elizabethan times by the fact that young boys played the parts of women, and that, in the case of Viola/Cesario, Shakespeare's plot calls for a boy actor to play the part of a young woman who then masquerades as a young man! In keeping with the spirit of comedy, Shakespeare was deliberately trying to be confusing and was challenging his audience to match wits with him.

Then there are the numerous plots and subplots that Shakespeare has carefully and compactly interwoven into *Twelfth Night*. Many Shakespearean scholars consider this play to be the Bard's most perfect comedy precisely because of its complex construction. The complicated main plot focuses on the mistaken identity of the brother-sister twins, Viola and Sebastian, and their (mis)adventures in and out of love with Olivia (the countess) and Orsino (the duke). The central theme is both set off and enriched by a variety of subplots. There is, for example, the "gulling" and humiliation of the normally sober but ambitious Malvolio by the insouciant Maria. In yet another subplot—this one devised by Sir Toby Belch—Malvolio is duped into believing himself mad. A third subplot is Sir Toby's careful arranging of a duel between reluctant antagonists, the boastful Sir Andrew Aguecheek and the disguised Viola.

Feminists will be pleased to note that the prime "movers and doers" in this play are women: Viola and Maria. They are independent, strong-minded, and resourceful, in addition to having the more conventional attraction of beauty. It is primarily their creativity and agility in attempting to achieve their goals that move along the action of the play. With the exception of whimsical, prankish Sir Toby, the male characters in *Twelfth Night* tend to be passive and reactive. Moreover, the comedy of the subplots is generated by the pomposity of the male ego and involves various means of puncturing that pomposity. For instance, Malvolio's impudent ambition to become a nobleman and marry Olivia and Aguecheek's unsupported overconfidence render them blind to the plots to humiliate them.

In her essay, " 'Are you Mad? Or What Are You?': Revelry and Revelation in *Twelfth Night,*"Gayle Greene focuses on three aspects of the play. She begins with a description and analysis of the various elements of Shakespeare's comic technique, calling our attention to the songs, the drunken foolery, the verbal wit, and the physical movement of the characters. She then develops a scale ranging from wisdom and clarity to folly and madness, according to which she suggests that we rank individual characters of the play. Greene ends with a discussion of Shakespeare's use of awareness as a comic technique—or the discrepancy in awarenesses between the characters and the audience. An understanding of the way comic effects are derived from the difference between what we know is happening and what the characters think is happening will be useful in the study of other plays by Shakespeare.

LESSON ASSIGNMENTS

In order to get the most out of the specially designed introductory material and to appreciate the unique qualities of the play itself, Gayle Greene strongly recommends that you prepare yourself in the following manner:
- Read the synopsis of *Twelfth Night* in this guide.
- Read the text of *Twelfth Night*.
- Read " 'Are You Mad? or What Are You': Revelry and Revelation in *Twelfth Night*" by Gayle Greene in this guide.
- View the television production.
- Complete the Self-test at the end of this lesson.

LEARNING OBJECTIVES

After completing the reading assignments and viewing the televised drama production, you should be able to:
1. Determine the number of plots in *Twelfth Night*. Describe how they relate to each other dramatically and thematically.
2. The characters repeatedly call one another "fools" or "madmen" and do, in fact, exhibit behavior ranging from folly and madness to clarity and control. Describe and rank each character from least to most foolish and mad.
3. Identify those characters who grow during the course of the play and those who do not, and describe what is learned by those who grow.
4. Describe the various attitudes toward love expressed or represented by the characters of the play.
5. Discuss the appropriateness of the title and subtitle of the play.
6. Identify how the differing levels of the characters' awarenesses of events contribute to the comic effects of the play.

SYNOPSIS OF THE PLAY

ACT I

In his music-filled palace, DUKE ORSINO of Illyria is melancholy over his hopeless love for the beautiful OLIVIA, who has vowed to live in seclusion for seven years to mourn her brother's death.

On the seacoast, two shipwreck survivors, VIOLA and the ship's captain, plan their future. The Captain thinks that Viola's twin brother, SEBASTIAN, also escaped the wreck. Viola decides to disguise herself as a boy and seek employment as a page to Duke Orsino.

At Olivia's home, her uncle, SIR TOBY BELCH, is trying to cheer up the simple SIR ANDREW AGUECHEEK, who is depressed because Olivia has failed to respond to his wooing.

In the palace, Viola has become a boy named "CESARIO," and the Duke is so fond of his new page that Viola/Cesario is sent to plead his love to Olivia. Viola/Cesario, in an aside, reveals that she has fallen in love with the Duke.

Meanwhile, Olivia's fool, FESTE, returns home after an absence. MARIA, Olivia's handmaid, warns Feste that Olivia is displeased. Olivia herself enters with her pompous, self-important steward, MALVOLIO, who denounces Feste, but Olivia defends him.

Viola/Cesario enters and speaks exquisitely of Duke Orsino's great love for Olivia. After "Cesario" leaves, Olivia discovers that she has fallen in love with the "boy" and sends Malvolio after Viola/Cesario with a ring, which she claims the "page" left behind.

ACT II

Viola's brother, SEBASTIAN, sure that Viola is dead and that an evil fate pursues him, refuses to take ANTONIO, a captain, as a companion. They separate, but Antonio vows to follow.

Meanwhile, Malvolio catches up with Viola/Cesario and tries to return the ring, which Viola/Cesario refuses.

Later, Sir Toby, Sir Andrew, and Feste are enjoying a noisy, drunken evening when Malvolio haughtily informs them that they will be evicted unless they reform. They hatch a plot against him: Maria will forge a letter in her mistress's handwriting, indicating that Olivia is in love with the steward.

Duke Orsino tells his new "page" of his love for Olivia, and after Feste sings a melancholy song, orders "Cesario" to return to Olivia.

In the meantime, the conspirators watch from concealment as Malvolio finds the forged letter. Malvolio believes every word and Sir Toby is so delighted that he decides to propose to Maria.

ACT III

In their second meeting, Viola/Cesario woos Olivia for Orsino, and Olivia confesses her love for "Cesario." Viola/Cesario can only say that she loves no woman and never will. Meanwhile, Sir Toby and FABIAN persuade Sir Andrew that he can win Olivia's favor by challenging "Cesario" to a duel.

In town, Sebastian discovers that Antonio has followed him; Antonio gives him money, and they agree to meet at an inn.

Malvolio has commenced his "wooing" of Olivia: smiling insipidly, dressed in hideous yellow stockings, and babbling absolute nonsense. Olivia, thinking he has gone mad, asks Sir Toby to deal with the lunatic. Malvolio is locked in a dark room, and Sir Andrew goes off to ambush "Cesario."

"Cesario" is surprised to learn from Sir Toby that Sir Andrew wants to duel with him. The two terrified duelists are brought together and quaking, draw their swords.

Suddenly, Antonio enters and (mistaking "Cesario" for the twin Sebastian) offers to duel in his place. Immediately, several peace officers arrive and arrest Antonio. Viola/Cesario now has hope that her brother may be alive.

ACT IV

Sir Andrew attacks Sebastian, thinking he is fighting "Cesario." Olivia stops the fight, also mistaking Sebastian for "Cesario," and invites him into the house.

Meanwhile, Feste imitates the local parson and torments Malvolio even further.

In the house, Sebastian is amazed (and delighted) at Olivia's apparent love for him, and agrees to marry her. Olivia, afraid that "Cesario" will change his mind again, brings in a priest and arranges a secret marriage on the spot.

ACT V

After the confusion of mistaken identities comes to a head, Sebastian appears and the twins are seen together for the first time. Olivia learns that she has wed the brother of "Cesario," and the Duke proposes marriage to his now-revealed page. Sir Toby has married Maria, making three pairs of newlyweds.

The plot against Malvolio is explained, and all misunderstandings and resentments are resolved—except for Malvolio's. The play closes with a melancholy song from Feste.

"Are You Mad? Or What Are You?"
Revelry and Revelation in *Twelfth Night*

Gayle Greene

Twelfth Night, or What You Will, is one of Shakespeare's most effective plays in performance. With its array of unforgettable comic characters, its scenes of high, boisterous hilarity, and its fabulous story of shipwreck, separated twins, mistaken identities, and romance, it offers something for everyone—"what you will." If this subtitle suggests the play's wide popular appeal, the main title associates it with holiday, the twelfth and last night of Christmas, an occasion of revelry when ordinary rules were reversed or relaxed, for which *Twelfth Night* may first have been performed, in 1601 or 1602.

The song, dance, drunkenness, and fooling that make for great fun on stage, however, may make for certain difficulties in reading, since they place a burden on the reader's imagination to construct the stage business, which becomes dazzlingly complicated in the final scenes, and to be alert, throughout, for lines that function as stage directions—like Sir Toby's "A plague o' this pickle-herring!" (I, v, 115), the cue to a resounding belch, true to his name and state most of the time. Indeed, Sir Toby Belch is the spirit of revelry who presides over this "merry world" (III, i, 95), who turns time topsy-turvy, making every day a holiday. With his famous challenge to Malvolio—"Dost thou think, because thou art virtuous, there shall be no more cakes and ale?" (II, iii, 105–6)—he expresses the spirit that wins out in this world. It is true to this spirit that the play's most sober of citizens, Malvolio, should be subjected to the most extreme indignity, confinement to a "dark house" as treatment for madness.

The scenes with these antics alternate with the love plots: two, or perhaps three or four, depending on whether we count the illusory and unrequited attachments that motivate much of the action. Orsino loves Olivia but Olivia loves "Cesario"; Cesario (actually Viola, who is wooing Olivia for Orsino) loves Orsino, thereby completing the circle, or triangle, but leaving everyone unsatisfied. The love plots all hinge on and are confused by Viola's disguise, which makes everything other than what it seems—as only she and we know. In a pattern typical to comedy, things become worse before they get better, reaching maximum complication when subplot entangles with main plot. At this point, Sebastian, Viola's missing twin, wanders into both plots, becoming embroiled in the duel Sir Toby has engineered between Cesario and Sir Andrew Aguecheek and becoming the object of Olivia's love. Mistaken for Cesario, Sebastian is physically assaulted and married within three scenes. But, as the focus of these confusions, Sebastian is also the means of their clarification, for, with his appearance, Olivia's love can find a more proper object; and, with Viola's identity revealed, Orsino's love, too, can settle appropriately. As identities are revealed and brother and sister are reunited, lovers can be properly paired and love requited; and the characters, formerly three, now four, can recombine in an order satisfactory to everyone. From the "dark house" of error and confusion, we emerge, with these revelations, to "the air" and "the glorious sun" (IV, iii, 1).

This movement through complication to clarification may be understood, like the play's antics, in relation to its association with holiday. Twelfth Night was one of the numerous Elizabethan holidays, liturgical, seasonal celebrations whose riotous festivities actually affirmed the return to the everyday reality they temporarily suspended, strengthening and clarifying the rules by going beyond them.[1] Besides being the culmination of Christmas revelry, Twelfth Night was the Feast of Epiphany, which commemorated the revelation of Christ to the Three Kings. Though the play makes no specific reference to this religious occasion, it does bear a more general relation to "epiphany" in the wider sense—of the manifestation or clarification of the essential nature of something. The happy endings conventional to comedy have resonances beyond their immediate contexts, suggesting the movement from a world where, as Feste quips, "nothing that is so is so" (IV, i, 8) to one where "that that is is" (IV, ii, 14). Shakespeare uses the familiar devices of comedy—disguise, mistaken identities, farcical confusions, and incongruities—to raise deeper issues of knowledge and reality.

The characters repeatedly call one another "mad" or "foolish"—"Foolery, sir, does walk about the orb like the sun; it shines everywhere" (II, i, 37–38). These words and their variants, "folly," "fooling," "madly," "madman," "madness," echo throughout; and "fool" has at least two senses, "simpleton" and "clown," and is used as a verb as well as a noun. The dialogue resounds with related words, "lunatic," "gull," "zany," "giddy," "frenzy," "fancy," "dream," and "distract"; "wit," "witty," "wise," and "reason" also occur, to suggest other possibilities, though they hardly balance this array. Malvolio's protest against being "exorcised" ("I am no more mad than you are" [IV, ii, 47]) defeats itself by its very standard of comparison, a "you" that includes a practicing fool (Feste), an actual fool (Andrew), and a drunk (Toby)—the "three wise men" of this play; and Feste rightly concludes, "Then you are mad indeed" (IV, ii, 87). Though Malvolio is not mad in the way his tormentors pretend, possessed by the devil, the play raises the question whether he is mad in any other sense.

Underlying the hijinks is an inquiry into the nature of folly and madness implying an obverse question concerning the "wisdom" or "wit" that enables one to see things as they are. An analysis of the characters' relations to "wisdom" or "folly," their capacities for clarity or confusion, reveals that knowledge and delusion are primary means of differentiating character as well as central themes. One of Shakespeare's most festive comedies, *Twelfth Night* is also one of his most profound, in its inquiry into problems of self and perception—how who we are and what we "will" determine what we see. Related to the concern with knowledge is the concern with love, which is central to this play, as to other of Shakespeare's romantic comedies, where it is similarly associated with madness. That problems of perception may be compounded by love is suggested by the various meanings of the word *will* in the subtitle, which could mean "wish" or "inclination," but could also mean the desire related to passion, the faculty traditionally opposed to reason. If "love is merely a madness," as Rosalind calls it (*As You Like It* [III, ii, 376]), and if passion alters perspective, we should expect considerable confusion in a play where most of the major characters are in love.

Our first indication of this problem is provided by Orsino's opening lines—"If music be the food of love, play on" (I, i, 1)—an evocation of "sweet sound" (I, i, 5) and "odor" (I, i, 7) intended by the noble Duke as expression of exalted longings. Craving "excess" of this "food" that, "surfeiting,/The appetite may sicken, and so die" (I, i, 2–3), Orsino's images work, in several ways, to undermine the sublimity of sentiment he intends, suggesting a rift between the illusion and actuality of his feelings that creates a discrepancy between his perspective and ours. Orsino is languishing in melancholy, luxuriating in its expression as in a warm bath, more involved with his own ideas than with Olivia—as his association of "fancy" (love) with the "fantastical" (imaginary) indicates (I, i, 14–15). We learn, also, that the object of these desires is not a woman who returns them, but one who has vowed to confine herself, like a cloistress, for seven years, in mourning a brother. That Orsino actually approves of this resolve suggests that this is precisely the sort of melodramatic gesture to which he himself is inclined. This scene ends, not with Orsino's moving toward Olivia, nor even resolving to win her, but in a drifting "away . . . to sweet beds of flow'rs" and "love-thoughts . . . canopied with bow'rs" (I, i, 41–42). Since it takes him four acts even to venture forth to woo her, his is not an attraction that risks the test of reality; thus it can remain on an idealized plane, though one might question whether it is love of anything but self. Orsino's physical inaction is also a psychological condition, emblematic of confinement within, and indulgence of, self.

Into this claustrophobic scene and stalemated situation, Viola enters like a breath of fresh air, announcing herself in a different idiom: "What country, friends, is this?" (I, ii, 1). Her response to what seems a brother's death ("perchance he is not drowned" [I, ii, 5]), her determination to get on with life, comments on the morbidity of Olivia's protracted mourning and reveals the system of parallels and contrasts on which the play is constructed. Shipwrecked and swept ashore, she comes from a sea that seems fresh and lifegiving, compared to the all-devouring force imagined by Orsino (I, i, 11–14).

The series of questions with which she considers various alternatives—"And what should I do in Illyria?" (I, ii, 3)—defines her as a woman of action, who will use time in a way that contrasts to Olivia's careless casting away of seven years of her youth; though her resignation to "time" (I, ii, 60) indicates understanding of the limits that circumscribe her. Viola is prompted to the idea of disguise by observing the integrity of the captain, whose "mind," she decides "suits/With [his] fair outward character" (I, ii, 50–51), and by her reflection that people's appearances are often at variance with their actual natures. The disguise she assumes will do much to compound such problems of perception for everyone in the play, generating the multiple confusions that are the heart of its comedy. Still, Viola's role-playing is simple and deliberate, compared to Orsino's stickier self-dramatizing, and so can become the means of restoring these characters, who are enmeshed in their fantasies, to a sense of reality.

The comic subplot characters we meet in the next scene, whose "caterwauling" is crazily incongruous to a household supposedly in mourning, introduce us to more extreme follies and deliberate deceptions. Sir Toby keeps Sir Andrew Aguecheek around for a drinking companion, for amusement, but primarily for his three thousand ducats a year. Sir Toby drains Andrew of his money by stuffing Andrew's self-esteem, encouraging him to believe himself a handsome and learned knight worthy of the hand of Olivia. The gallant appearance conjured by Toby's imagination is at odds with the actuality we can construct from the dialogue: hair that "hangs like flax" (I, iii, 91), a thin face (V, i, 199), and sallowness of complexion suggested by the name (*ague* means "fever" or "illness"). The reputation for learning Toby fabricates for Andrew is similarly belied by Andrew's difficulty with the word "accost" (I, iii, 54). While most of the characters in this play move easily between literal and figurative levels of language in wordplay and puns, Andrew seems to have trouble finding one meaning per word. We laugh at him rather than with him—a silly fool bogged down at a literal level of reality, who knows neither who nor what he is, nor most of what goes on around him. Generally, the less a character understands and the further our perspective is distanced from his, the more our laughter is directed *at* him; the more he knows and the more closely our perspectives are allied, the more we laugh *with* him;[2] so that, besides being a central theme and measure of character, delusion is a major source of comic effect. But some rays of self-recognition penetrate Andrew's obtuseness, as he confesses occasional doubt about the quality of his "wit" (I, iii, 77); and the wistfulness of "I was adored once" (II, iii, 167) indicates that his aspiration for Olivia may be tinged by a desire for love.

It is typical of the reversals of seeming and being in this world that its official jester, its "allowed fool" (I, v, 89), is actually its shrewdest character—formidable in his wit, wordplay, and powers of observation. Feste is, as Viola understands, "wise enough to play the fool" (III, i, 58), but is as clear as she is about the difference between role and reality: "I wear not motley in my brain" (I, v, 51–52); and she is best able to appreciate the "wit," "observation," and timing required of his role (III, i, 59–61) because she understands the exigencies of her own.

In the scene where Feste first appears, at the end of Act I, we see the way his responses to others and theirs to him illuminate their characters. Within a few lines, he calls Toby a fool ("a drunken man" is "like a drowned man, a fool, and a madman" [I, v, 124–25]) and "proves" Olivia one, for mourning a brother whom she supposes in heaven (I, v, 67). And, in fact, he zeroes in on aspects of both these characters that qualify them for places in the pageant of foolery. Though Toby is sufficiently lucid to manipulate others, his perpetual drunkenness makes him as often the object as the instigator of laughter. And Olivia's determination to mourn seven years is excessive to the point of foolishness, though she shows herself capable of more than folly in this dialogue, as she is lured out, in spite of herself, into amused engagement with Feste: "What think you of this fool, Malvolio? Doth he not mend?" (I, v, 69). Her rebuke of Malvolio's stern, humorless response exactly describes him, in terms that relate his warped perception to his warped character: "O, you are sick of self-love, Malvolio, and taste with a distempered appetite. To be generous, guiltless, and of free disposition, is to take those things for birdbolts that you deem cannon bullets" (I, v, 85–88). One of the Fool's functions is to show the difference between those who can laugh and those who cannot; and in this scene we see that the ability to laugh at oneself may be a further measure of character.

Feste and Viola are the only characters who go between the two plots and locales of the play, Orsino's and Olivia's households. This freedom of movement is emblematic of their "free dispositions," though it is also significant that they must go in disguise. By the beginning of the second act, Viola has linked the two plots, arriving at Olivia's household in suit for Orsino. From here on, the love plot, which turns on Olivia's infatuation with her, and the comic subplot, which turns on the gulling of Malvolio, offer further variations of the types of confusions encountered in the course of the first act: confusions that originate in character interact with confusions created by circumstance, to be further compounded by deliberate fooling.

The gulling of Malvolio is a more extreme version of the gulling of Andrew. Both are deliberate deceptions practiced on inflated self-images that hold out Olivia as bait, but Malvolio's turns on a self-deception so complete that it verges on "madness." Maria, Olivia's shrewd, fun-loving maid, gets the inspiration for driving him mad when he bursts in on their carousing with "are you mad? Or what are you?" (II, iii, 80). She pinpoints exactly the quality that makes him vulnerable: "an affectioned [affected] ass . . . the best persuaded of himself; so crammed, as he thinks, with excellencies that it is his grounds of faith that all that look on him love him" (II, iii, 135–39). Malvolio is another who, not knowing himself, does not see things as they are.

But Malvolio hardly needs their device to make an ass of himself, already deep, as he is, in his fantasies, "practicing behavior to his . . . shadow" (II, v, 15), in the scene where he finds the letter. Though the letter resists him in a few particulars, he pieces out "Malvolio" from "M, O, A, I" (II, v, 127) and "crushes" (II, v, 128) its meaning to his "will"—an "ill will," as his name indicates. What makes him worse than the others is the arrogance with which he exempts himself from the human condition— "Go hang yourselves, all! You are idle shallow things; I am not of your element" (III, iv, 115–16)— and the purely mercenary nature of his aspiration for Olivia. His desire for her is motivated, not by love or attraction, only by ambition for position and power over "the lighter people" (V, i, 329). Cut off from love or understanding of others, he becomes the object of their derision and manipulation. Malvolio's confinement to a "dark house" is appropriate expression of where he has been all along, locked in a nature "dark as hell" (IV, ii, 46), an egotism unlit by self recognition, humility, or humor.

Olivia's plight, like Malvolio's, results from self-delusion in conjunction with external deception, except that Viola's masquerade as Cesario creates confusions contrary to her intentions which, within a scene, cause Olivia to go back on her intentions as well. Olivia's infatuation with Viola/Cesario divides her "will" from her reason—"I do I know not what" (I, v, 294)—and only we and Viola know how much more she does know, how totally her confusions take in the external reality (of Cesario's identity) and the internal reality (of her own feelings). Though her attachment is more hopeless than Orsino's for her and results in a solution more uneasy than comic, Olivia's transfer of affection from a dead brother to a living being may be a positive movement, for a personality so cautious and convoluted, in the reaching out and risk-taking required in love.

Viola's response to Olivia's advances combines sharp criticism with gentle tact. Whereas Andrew is too dense to recognize his own case in the gulling of Malvolio, Viola is sufficiently self-aware to understand and sympathize with others. Knowing "I am not that I play" (I, v, 176), she can discern the subtler confusions of Olivia: "You do think you are not what you are" (III, i, 136). Her own sorrow makes her sensitive to the unrequited longings of both lovers she goes between, and enables her to act as a kind of tutor, especially to Orsino, in matters of love and reality. In the poignant scene where Viola comes closest to confessing her feelings—with her tale, "my father had a daughter loved a man" (II, iv, 106)—she tries to make Orsino stretch his sympathies to imagine a woman who might love him as much as he does Olivia. Her remonstrance, "But if she [Olivia] cannot love you, sir?" (II, iv, 86), is a needed reminder that other people exist, and her advice that love does not depend on his will alone, that it consists more of deeds than vows

(II, iv, 115–17), shows how well she knows him. Orsino's response—"I cannot be so answered (II, iv, 87)—denies that mutuality of response is essential to love, but Viola urges, and demonstrates by example, that it is. Whereas he, in his word-spinning, confounds the rhetoric with the reality of love, she remains silent about her feelings, but acts on them, performing the most difficult of sacrifices, wooing another woman for him. She is constrained from more direct expression or action, however, by her very sense of the limits she urges, sensitivity to his feelings. But Orsino's response in this dialogue, as he is drawn into sympathetic engagement with her, hints at his better potential and their developing friendship.

One function of her disguise is to allow for this intimacy, which would have been difficult between unmarried women and men in the Renaissance.

Our perspective is more closely allied with Viola's than with any other character's because she knows the most. She understands more even than Feste, not only because she knows what he cannot, the truth of her identity, but also because she is emotionally involved with her world in a way he is not. Feste may be as observant of others and have a salutary effect on them, by making them laugh; but he takes little part in the action, does not love, and is not included in the pairings of the resolution. The combination of clarity and feeling that enables Viola to draw egocentric, self-absorbed personalities out of themselves makes her representative of what is best in her world. It usually happens in Shakespeare's comedies that this educating, nurturing role is the woman's; but we should ask whether the qualities that give Viola this power are uniquely "feminine"—that is, those society ascribes to women—or whether traditionally "feminine" qualities of instinctive sympathy and self-sacrifice are combined with self-reliance and a grasp of reality usually attributed to men.

An androgynous ideal of character and behavior is suggested by Viola's playing the role of a boy—a disguise rendered more complicated by the fact that a boy actor is actually playing the part of Viola. While the role-playing of the others confines them in self, Viola's actually extends the boundaries of self, enabling her to express the best of both sexes. Viola is integrated in a way no one else in the play is, combining the capacity for love and knowledge, the strengths of "maid and man" (V, i, 225), in "one heart . . . one truth" (III, i, 155). Perhaps this is why she is the only one of the three major characters who remains constant in her love throughout the play.

Yet even Viola is not always clear about what is happening. Though she sees more than anyone else, things are often beyond her control and occasionally beyond her comprehension. No one in the play sees as much as we do, most see considerably less. This discrepancy in levels of awareness—between what we know is happening and what the characters think is happening—is the source of rich comic effect.[3]

Act, III, scene iv, where subplot entangles with main plot, is particularly abundant in such effects, involving nearly all the characters in the play in actions none of them fully understands. Olivia, laboring under misconceptions concerning Cesario and herself, sends for the "sad," "civil" (III, iv, 4) Malvolio to calm her. He, under layers of delusion concerning himself, her, and reality generally, enters madly costumed, maniacally smiling, winking, and blowing kisses, imagining that this behavior will win her. The horrified Olivia concludes that he is mad, but his egotism makes him so impervious that he construes all her responses as verifying what he "wills." From this exchange, which would be incomprehensible to anyone not privy to his confusions, the scene moves to the duel Toby has contrived between Andrew and Viola, a contest neither can win, but neither can refuse without giving away the shams of their disguises—Andrew's as gallant and Viola's as man. Our laughter and their consternation stem from the gap between their roles and realities, which Toby has effectively widened, by fabricating fierce fighting reputations for each. This action leads to a mistaken identity of another sort, when Antonio, Sebastian's friend, takes Cesario for Sebastian, intervenes to defend him, and gets called mad and hauled away. To twist Maria's terms, slightly, "some are born fools, some achieve folly, and some have folly thrust upon them"—and all interact in this scene, butting up against one another in comic ignorance, in a fugue of error and confusion.

As these complications proliferate, they assume almost a life of their own, beyond any of the characters' comprehension or control, so that it does, indeed, seem, as Feste quips, that, "nothing that is so is so"; and nothing short of a miracle can set things right. Sebastian's appearance, simultaneous with Viola's, provides such a miracle; the action is stilled, the dialogue slowed, as brother and sister stand in stunned contemplation of one another, and all pause in amazement at what seems a wonder. Paradoxically, what seems the bifurcation of one being into two—"One face, one voice, one habit, and two persons—/A natural perspective that is and is not" (V, i, 208–9)[4]—provides the means of bringing things together. Incongruity is at the heart of this comedy—between illusion and actuality, the characters' intentions and acts, their awarenesses and ours. These incongruities, and the psychological and philosophical perplexities in which the characters are embroiled, are resolved in a glorious revelation of love regained that makes all odds even. As two are made one in relationships of marriage, family, and friendship, the movement from division to union, from confusion to certainty—to a world where "that that is is"—is accomplished. Not everyone is included in the harmony of the conclusion: Malvolio takes up an uncomfortably large portion of the final scene, to storm out, in the end, as ignorant and malevolent as ever, understanding nothing of what has happened and vowing revenge. But the reconciliations and reunions toward which the play moves provide an image of the underlying unity of a benign providential order—of "tempests [that] are kind, and salt waves fresh in love" (III, iv, 364).

An analysis of the characters in terms of their awareness has revealed the values Shakespeare builds into the play. Wisdom involves wit, clarity, the complexity of perspective that enables one to discern appearances from actualities, roles from realities, and literal from figurative meanings of language. But wisdom involves qualities of character as well as mind: an ability to love related to an ability to laugh, and the integrity and integration that derive from self-knowledge. Whereas folly and its more extreme form, madness, consist of enmeshment in self and illusion, "to be generous, guiltless, and of free disposition" is to see clearly, feel deeply, combine good sense with open-heartedness. Since those at the lowest levels of awareness are the most thoroughly enmeshed, "free disposition" is related to freedom: though all in this play depend on great good luck to bring things right, and wisdom consists partly in understanding the limits to what can be comprehended or controlled. But "thought is free" (I, iii, 63), as Maria says early on, if not to determine events, free for the joyful acceptance of present reality and faith in the future that the play affirms.[5]

Love is not "madness," though some of its aberrant forms may resemble madness. True love is a reaching out to and recognition of another that depends on self-knowledge and acceptance—sane, rare, and difficult. Orsino grows out of his infatuation with Olivia, a sentimental and affected longing for an unattainable ideal, into a mature feeling for Viola based on knowledge and mutuality. Lest we too ponderously turn the play to philosophy, however, we should recall that it is a comedy that contains some "improbable" fictions (III, iv, 120), Olivia's sudden switch to Sebastian being one of them. But even this switch has its own psychological validity as Olivia's progress from attachment to a being of the same sex to a masculine version of that being, in the development of mature heterosexual love.

As Feste's answer to the question posed by his song indicates, love is related to time: "What is love? 'Tis not hereafter;/Present mirth hath present laughter" (II, iii, 44–45). Love is, like laughter, "present"—not in some vague, unrealized future—and the characters may be differentiated according to their ability to understand or to learn this. Olivia's determination to spend seven years of her youth mourning the past indicates an emotional stagnation like Orsino's. Her "waste" of the time is rebuked by the striking of the clock (III, i, 127); her complacent claim that her beauty "will endure" (I, v, 224) is refuted by Feste's claim to the contrary, "Youth's a stuff will not endure" (II, iii, 49); and her restoration to reality involves an education, like Orsino's, in appreciating what is given by the present—which is, luckily for her, as for him, an attractive, living being who returns her love. Toby's ability to enjoy the present joins him in the spirit of fun with Maria. Yet his denial of past and future shows an obliviousness, like his niece's, to time's real effects; and his commitment to Maria, a woman who can "confine" him better than he confines himself (I, iii, 7–8), involves some coming to terms with the uses of time. Antithetical to Toby in this respect, as in others, is Malvolio, "a kind of Puritan" (II, iii, 128), whose tightness with time is one with his inability to love, who learns as little about these matters as he does about anything else. Somewhere between the extremes of extravagance and hoarding is a wise acknowledgment that time must be used, but cannot be forced, an acceptance of the present that allows for knowledge and love—exemplified, like other wisdoms, in Viola.

Feste's final song, however, provides another point of view on the relation of time to life, which brings to the surface the undercurrent of melancholy—the sense of time's presence and passing—evoked by such songs as "What Is Love?" and the haunting "Come Away Death." Feste's panorama of the stages of life in a world "begun" "a great while ago" (V, i, 394) alters the perspective with the effect of a camera panning out, dwarfing and diminishing the arena of human action. Revelry does not thrive in this song, nor does anything else; youth, manhood, marriage, old age, succeed one another futilely, passing so quickly that all blur meaninglessly, jumbled together with "foolish things" (V, i, 380) and "tosspots" (V, i, 392). Feste's conclusion has puzzled and disturbed critics, both for its meaning and its relation to the preceding action, since it seems to express a sense of time contrary to that suggested by the play as a whole. But if an awareness of life's mutability can result in an eagerness to seize the day, which, Shakespeare suggests, is wisdom for the characters, it may also result, with the change in perspective accomplished by Feste, in the questioning of the value of any effort. Giving Feste this last word, Shakespeare implies that the concord of the final scene that "golden time convents" (V, i, 371) may be tenuous. Nothing can endure the "rain" evoked by Feste's repeated refrain, nor the chill "wind" that blasts in as though from eternity.

As the last night of the holy season, the twelfth night of Christmas included revelry and revelation—but it also suggested an end to the revels. This sense of finality is corroborated by the position of *Twelfth Night* in Shakespeare's development, as the last of his romantic comedies. Shakespeare's next plays would be tragedies whose protagonists, like King Lear and Othello, are blind to the realities of themselves or of others and act out their errors with tragic consequences. The delusion and misconstruings that are comic in this play turn tragic there; consequences that thwart intentions lead to tragic conclusions in plays where no good luck intervenes, no benign providence orders things happily. A transitional play, *Twelfth Night* combines the subject of comedy, love, with the focus on knowledge and reality central to the great tragedies that follow, where madness becomes clinical and delusion turns fatal. The next time we hear Feste's song, it is sung by another wise and bitter fool, desperately accompanying the ravings of his mad master, King Lear, in an actual tempest on a heath. The happiness achieved by *Twelfth Night* is still a possibility here, but seems increasingly precarious, in the gathering storm, "the wind and the rain" of Feste's last song.

ANNOTATED BIBLIOGRAPHY

Barber, C. L. "Testing Courtesy and Humanity in *Twelfth Night.*" In his *Shakespeare's Festive Comedy: A Study of Dramatic Form and Its Relation to Social Custom.* Princeton: Princeton University Press, 1972.
This indispensable study relates Shakespearean comedy, structurally and atmospherically, to Elizabethan holidays. The twelve nights of Christmas, a time of feasting within doors in the cold season, presided over by a Lord of Misrule, were particularly full of "the rough pleasures of defiance and mockery" (p. 24). Barber analyzes the antagonism between Malvolio and the "lighter people" (V, i, 329) in terms of class conflict, Malvolio's ambitions representing the new forces of capitalism and Protestantism that would eventually triumph over the idle but gracious aristocracy.

Evans, Bertrand. "The Fruits of the Sport: *Twelfth Night.*" In his *Shakespeare's Comedies,* pp. 118–43. London: Oxford University Press, 1960.
Evans analyzes the effects of comedy in terms of Shakespeare's exploitation of discrepancies among the awarenesses of participants and between the awarenesses of participants and audience. *Twelfth Night,* a "rich pattern of practices, cunningly interwoven" (p. 118), represents the culmination of Shakespeare's use of this technique. "Seven of the principal persons are active practisers, and they operate six devices . . . and the effects of the play arise from the exploitation of the gaps [in awareness] they open." "The awarenesses in *Twelfth Night* are so structured that an overpeerer gloating in his advantage is usually overpeered by another participant or by us" (pp. 118–19).

King, Walter N., ed. *Twentieth Century Interpretations of "Twelfth Night."* Englewood Cliffs, N.J.: Prentice-Hall, 1968.
This useful collection of critical studies includes especially interesting essays by Joseph H. Summers ("The Masks of *Twelfth Night*"), Porter Williams, Jr. ("Mistakes in *Twelfth Night* and Their Resolution: A Study in Some Relationships of Plot and Theme"), and G. K. Hunter ("Plot and Subplot in *Twelfth Night*").

Leggatt, Alexander. *Shakespeare's Comedy of Love.* London: Methuen Inc., 1974. (New York: Barnes and Noble Books, 1974.)
This work is a rich and suggestive exploration of Shakespeare's romantic comedies in terms of their combination of disparate elements—"realistic" and "stylized." The recognizable social types of the comic subplot in *Twelfth Night* are juxtaposed to the stylized, courtly aristocratic characters of the main plot.

Novy, Marianne. " 'And You Smile Not, He's Gagged': Mutuality in Shakespearean Comedy." *Philological Quarterly* 55 (1976):178–94.

Novy discusses Shakespeare's lovers and jesters as needing responses from others to affirm their identities. Feste taunts Malvolio, in the passage quoted in the title of the essay, for faulting him for his dependence on audience response, but the joking exchanges with which he draws his listeners out of themselves are analogous to the lovers' development out of static, unrequited longings into relationships based on mutuality.

Traversi, D. A. *"Twelfth Night."* In his *An Approach to Shakespeare,* Vol. I, pp, 329–49. New York: Doubleday, 1969.

Traversi pays particular attention to language and verse in relation to the other elements—character, motive, action—that make up the dramatic reality of a play. "The 'serious' part of *Twelfth Night* deals primarily with conceptions of romantic love derived from the literary taste, aristocratic, and sophisticated, of the day" (p. 329). "The comic scenes in prose" provide a "reflection of the underside of that aristocratic life . . . a decayed feudal order" (p. 341). The restoration of harmony in the final scene looks forward to the symbolic transformations of Shakespeare's last plays, *The Winter's Tale* and *The Tempest.*

Notes

1. C. L. Barber's excellent work, *Shakespeare's Festive Comedy: A Study of Dramatic Form in Its Relation to Social Custom* (Princeton: Princeton University Press, 1972) analyzes the structure and atmosphere of Shakespeare's comedies in relation to Elizabethan holidays.
2. Joseph H. Summers, "The Masks of *Twelfth Night" (The University Review* 22, 1955; reprinted in *Twentieth Century Interpretations of "Twelfth Night,"* ed. Walter N. King [Englewood Cliffs, N.J.: Prentice-Hall, 1968], 15–23) divides the characters into those we laugh at and those we laugh with, according to whether they know or do not know what roles they are playing.
3. For Shakespeare's use of this technique of "discrepant awareness," see Bertrand Evans, *Shakespeare's Comedies* (London: Oxford University Press, 1960).
4. Walter N. King notes, in his introduction to *Twentieth Century Interpretation of "Twelfth Night"* (Englewood Cliffs, N.J.: Prentice-Hall, 1968), that "perspective" has both the technical, Renaissance sense, of a picture or figure constructed to produce a fantastic effect, and the more general significance it has today, meaning "point of view," which suggests the change in viewpoint experienced by the major characters in their educations.
5. Derek Traversi's discussion of the significance of the "awakenings" in this scene is particularly good. *An Approach to Shakespeare,* vol. I (New York: Doubleday, 1969), p. 339.

SELF-TEST

Multiple-choice Questions

1. Which character is in love for love's sake?
   a. Malvolio
   b. Orsino
   c. Sebastian
   d. Olivia
   e. Viola
2. Which of the following is *not* a central theme of *Twelfth Night?*
   a. folly versus wisdom
   b. seeming versus being
   c. madness versus sanity
   d. lust versus temperance
3. Which of the following characters is *least* foolish or mad?
   a. Malvolio
   b. Sir Toby
   c. Orsino
   d. Olivia
   e. Viola
4. Throughout most of the play the relationship between Viola, Orsino, and Olivia can be said to be
   a. a vicious circle.
   b. a love triangle.
   c. a menage á trois.
   d. unfriendly at best.
5. Which of the following sets of characters do *not* find lovemates by the end of the play?
   a. Sir Toby and Sir Andrew
   b. Sebastian and Sir Toby
   c. Sir Andrew and Orsino
   d. Malvolio and Orsino
   e. Malvolio and Sir Andrew
6. Who said the following passage to whom?
   "My father had a daughter loved a man
   As it might be perhaps, were I a woman
   I should your lordship . . ."
   a. Olivia to Orsino
   b. Olivia to Sebastian
   c. Viola to Orsino
   d. Maria to Sir Toby
   e. Orsino to Olivia
7. What is the irony of the passage cited in question 6?
   a. The person saying it is incapable of love.
   b. The "daughter" of the "father" is in reality a man.
   c. The "man" and the "father" are the same person.
   d. The "father" never had a daughter.
   e. The person saying it is a woman.

8. What kind of fool is Feste?
   a. ". . . a foolish wit . . ."
   b. ". . . a witty fool . . ."
   c. ". . . a fool's zany . . ."
   d. ". . . an affectioned ass . . ."
9. Viola's reaction when she realizes that Olivia has fallen in love with Cesario can be described as
   a. elated.
   b. jealous.
   c. bewildered.
   d. mournful.
10. Which of the following devices is *not* used by Shakespeare in *Twelfth Night?*
    a. separated twins
    b. mistaken identity
    c. song and dance
    d. banished nobility
    e. drunken revelry

Short-answer Essay Questions

1. Briefly explain why Feste can be termed the "shrewdest character in the play."
2. Describe what Malvolio and Sir Andrew have in common in terms of the way they are treated by Sir Toby.
3. Relate the holiday of Twelfth Night and Epiphany to the title and the overall action in *Twelfth Night*.
4. Explain the concept that "we laugh *at* characters who are ignorant and *with* those who are aware of the confusion in which they are embroiled" in terms of the characters in *Twelfth Night*.

Questions for Reflection

1. Describe the various attitudes toward love expressed or represented by the characters of the play. Compare that love with the type of love expressed or represented by the character with whom each character is coupled in Act V.
2. Identify which characters grow during the course of the play and which do not. Describe what is learned by those who grow.
3. Outline the various plots and subplots in *Twelfth Night*. Compare and contrast the central themes of each.
4. Discuss the appropriateness of the title and subtitle of the play in light of the fact that Twelfth Night is never celebrated nor mentioned in the play.

ANSWER KEY

Answers to Multiple-choice Questions

1. b (evidence throughout the play, especially I, i and II, ii; also essay)
2. d (evidence throughout the play; essay)
3. e (evidence throughout the play; essay)
4. a (evidence throughout the play; essay)
5. e (V, i)

6. c (II, iv)
7. c (II, iv)
8. b (I, v; essay)
9. c (II, ii)
10. d (evidence throughout the play; essay)

Suggested Answers to Short-answer Essay Questions

1. Feste is the most formidable in his wit. He never loses a wordplay duel and quickly and accurately observes and sizes up paradoxical situations and reveals them for all their irony and truth.
2. Both Malvolio and Sir Andrew are the gulls of plots largely engineered by Sir Toby. Malvolio is gulled by the phony letter, and Sir Andrew is gulled into hanging around Olivia's household (with his money, of course) in the hopes of winning Olivia's favor. Also, Sir Andrew is gulled out of his horse.
3. The title associates the play thematically with the twelfth and last night of Christmas, which was traditionally a time when ordinary rules were reversed or relaxed. Also, the play may have been first performed on Twelfth Night. The subtitle of the play, "What You Will," suggests that there is something in the play for everybody.
4. Malvolio and Sir Andrew are probably the most deluded, least aware characters in *Twelfth Night*. We laugh *at* their folly as they are tricked and maneuvered by other, more aware, characters. Viola and Feste are probably the most aware. We laugh *with* them since we both appreciate the humor or irony of the moment simultaneously.

THE TRAGEDY OF KING RICHARD THE SECOND

INTRODUCTION TO THE PLAY

William Shakespeare wrote ten history plays, but he did not write them all at one time, he did not write them in chronological order, and he left huge gaps in their historical sequence. Shakespeare's chronicles begin with *King John* in 1199 and conclude 334 years later with the birth of the future Queen Elizabeth in *Henry VIII*. In the process, he skips well over two hundred years of English history and the reign of seven different monarchs; moreover, he wrote the three parts of *Henry VI* five or six years before he wrote the two parts of *Henry IV*. Because Shakespeare wrote his history plays during the formative first half of his quarter-century career, there are significant changes in his literary style and dramatic technique between the first and last histories he wrote.

Richard II begins what Shakespeareans often refer to as the "Henriad," a series of four plays (a "tetralogy"), which follow each other chronologically, both historically and dramatically. With *1 Henry IV, 2 Henry IV,* and *Henry V,* the Henriad comprises a quartet of history plays renowned for their poetry, humanity, and keen understanding of the people who make history. (See the genealogical table in Figure 1 to understand the relationship among the principal characters of the plays of the Henriad.) The opening play focuses on the domestic dissension troubling England in 1398, the challenge of the Lancaster family led by Henry Bolingbroke, and the overthrow and murder of the vacillating King Richard II. *1 and 2 Henry IV* continue the story of the consolidation of the shaky Lancastrian hold on the throne under the practical but troubled Henry IV. In addition, they provide the background for the roisterous adventures of the prodigal heir-apparent, Prince Hal, and his dissolute companions, chief among whom is the inimitable Sir John Falstaff. These middle plays also show the maturing of Hal into a responsible statesman, all brought to fruition in the final play with the victory in France of the English forces at Agincourt under the heroic leadership of Henry V.

As you move through the four plays of the Henriad, you will notice that many of the same characters appear in them. The latter plays contain many references to persons and events dealt with in the previous dramas. Information is cumulative as the Henriad unfolds, prompting scholars to suggest that an appreciation of the latter plays is hampered without an understanding of the earlier plays. Fortunately, all four plays in the Henriad will be broadcast this

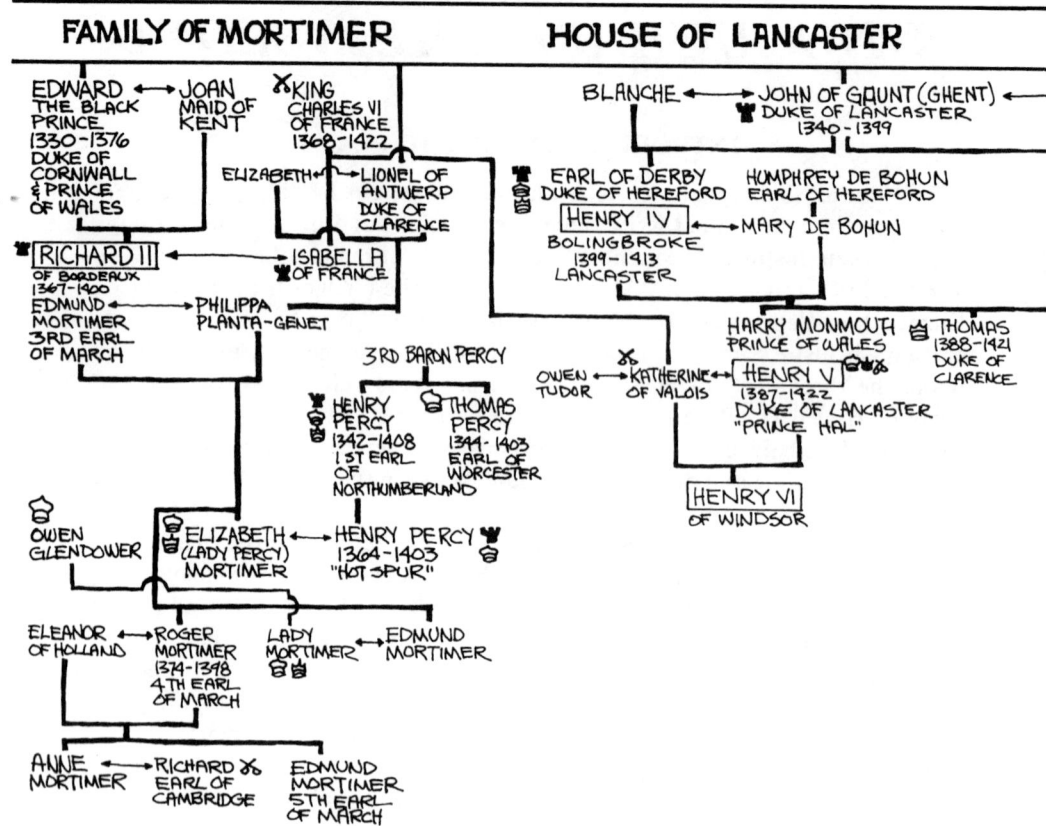

Figure 1. Genealogical table for the Henriad

The Tragedy of King Richard the Second

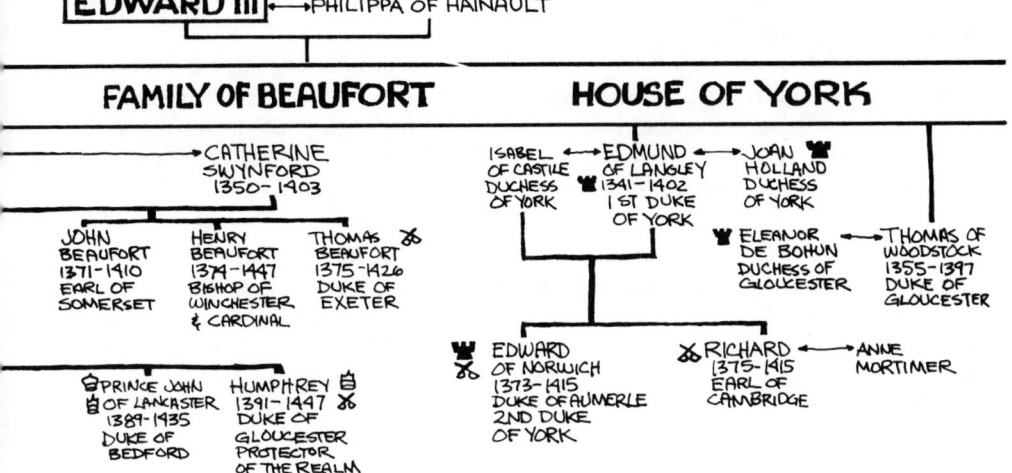

ENGLISH KINGS AND HISTORY PLAYS

PLAY	BORN-DIED	REIGNED	PLAY COVERS
RICHARD II	1367-1400	1377-1399	1398-1400
1 HENRY IV	1367-1413	1399-1413	1402-1403
2 HENRY IV	1367-1413	1399-1413	1403-1413
HENRY V	1387-1422	1413-1422	1414-1420

season, providing you with a rare opportunity to follow the entire tetralogy in proper sequence.

Richard II is set in 1398–1400, but the events in it continue quarrels, rivalries, and claims that, as Shakespeare's audience knew, had begun much earlier, and which would continue to shape history down to Shakespeare's own day. Much of the history of this period is obscure, and Shakespeare takes some liberties with what there is. Briefly, however, the events leading up to the opening of the play are as follows: Richard's grandfather, Edward III, had seven sons, the eldest of whom was Richard's father. Both father and grandfather died in quick succession, leaving Richard II king at the age of ten in 1377. After a long minority, governed by a council that included none of his uncles, Richard took power himself and ruled with the help of a number of court favorites and advisors.

Then, as now, the lure of fame, fortune, and power was strong, and during the first twenty years of Richard's reign various groups of nobles, including two of Richard's uncles—Gaunt and Gloucester—came into and out of favor with the king. The nobles' attempt to seize power from the king enjoyed some popular support, for Richard alienated his subjects by his extravagant high living, which he supported by seizing much of the wealth the nobles felt was theirs.

In 1397 Richard and his youngest uncle, Gloucester, fell out, and Gloucester, guarded by the Duke of Norfolk, was imprisoned to await trial. Gloucester died under mysterious circumstances and many—including Gaunt's son Bolingbroke—held Norfolk and Richard accountable. As the play begins, Bolingbroke accuses both Mowbray, Duke of Norfolk, and (indirectly) the King of complicity in the murder of Gloucester.

The play raises some important political questions but is, perhaps, most notable for its poetry and its portrayal of Richard's character. Professor Michael Mullin touches on both of these aspects of the play in his essay. His major concern, however, is to provide you with a way to approach not only this play but any play you wish to study, and you may want to use the exercises he outlines for *Richard II* with other plays in this course.

LESSON ASSIGNMENTS

In order to get the most out of the specially designed introductory material and to appreciate the unique qualities of the play itself, Michael Mullin strongly recommends that you prepare yourself in the following manner:
- Read *"Richard II:* An Experiment in Staging" by Michael Mullin in this guide.
- In his essay, Mullin will direct you to subsequent assignments at appropriate points.
- Complete the Self-test at the end of this lesson.

LEARNING OBJECTIVES

After completing the reading assignments and viewing the televised drama production, you should be able to:
1. Describe the ways in which Richard uses his public responsibility for personal advantage and discuss the consequences of these actions in the play.
2. Build a description of the physical movement in the play from the script and contrast that with the physical movement as portrayed in the television performance.
3. Evolve descriptions of the characters in the play from the text—both from their own parts and from the ways in which other characters talk about them.
4. Evolve a description of costumes and a list of props from the text of the play and discuss how these embody the central conflict of *Richard II.*
5. Distinguish between text and subtext and relate this distinction to the action of the play.

SYNOPSIS OF THE PLAY

ACT I

England, 1398: KING RICHARD II commands HENRY, Duke of HEREFORD (BOLINGBROKE) and Sir THOMAS MOWBRAY, Duke of NORFOLK, to settle a feud between them. King Richard and JOHN OF GAUNT, Bolingbroke's father, fail to reconcile them, and a time is set for the two knights to face one another in combat. At the tournament, Richard banishes both men from England.

Later, with his friends and advisors, Richard laughs at Bolingbroke's fate. When word comes that John of Gaunt is dying, Richard vows to confiscate Gaunt's wealth to finance an expedition against Ireland.

ACT II

The dying Gaunt lectures Richard for neglecting his royal duties. Furious, the King illegally seizes all of Gaunt's possessions the moment he learns the old man is dead—thus disinheriting Gaunt's son, Bolingbroke. Leaving the kingdom in the hands of his ineffectual uncle, the Duke of YORK, Richard sails for Ireland.

Almost immediately the Queen learns that Bolingbroke has returned and has been joined by the kingdom's most powerful nobles. When the Duke of York goes to meet the rebels, Bolingbroke declares that he only wants his inheritance returned.

ACT III

Bolingbroke, now in command, executes two of Richard's closest advisors, just as the King is landing on the coast of Wales. At first, Richard cannot believe that he might lose his throne—he is, he believes, God's appointed king—but as he learns of disaster after disaster, he despairs and dismisses his forces. Almost alone, he goes to Flint Castle, where Bolingbroke finds him. Despite Bolingbroke's claims that he is not trying to seize the crown, Richard realizes that he is Bolingbroke's prisoner and returns to London as a captive.

ACT IV

The final confrontation takes place before Parliament: Bolingbroke wants the crown, and Richard, although he knows he has no choice, cannot bear the idea of giving it up. Finally, however, he announces his decision to abdicate and a date is set for Bolingbroke's coronation as Henry IV. Richard is sent to the Tower of London, while a few loyal lords begin a plot to prevent Henry's overthrow.

ACT V

The Queen sees Richard for the last time; she is to be returned to France and he will be imprisoned. Meanwhile, the Duke of York learns that his son, AUMERLE, is plotting against the new king, Henry IV. The Duke goes before the King to denounce his own son, but Aumerle gets to him first and—with the help of his mother, the Duchess of York—he successfully pleads his case. Aumerle is forgiven, but orders are given to capture the other members of the plot.

Now the story—and the life—of King Richard move quickly toward an end. Sir Pierce Exton, having heard King Henry wish aloud for Richard's death, hurries to Pomfret Castle and kills Richard. When Henry learns of Richard's death, he is horrified; he banishes Exton and vows to go on a crusade to the Holy Land to atone for the murder.

Richard II: An Experiment in Staging

Michael Mullin

The aim of this guide is to help you enjoy and understand *The Tragedy of King Richard the Second*. It is not meant to summarize historical or literary scholarship—for that you can turn to other sources. Rather, I would like to give you some background information and some suggestions for reading and thought that my students at the University of Illinois, including those in last year's telecourse, have found helpful. In my classes we approach Shakespeare's plays the way people in the theater do—as scripts for performance. I don't mean that we try to get up an actual performance, but we do try to think of plays the way actors and directors do. We think of the plays as they exist in the theater, and this seems to me an especially good way to prepare for the viewing of the television broadcast. Although you may be tempted only to read through this guide and skip the exercises, be sure to complete them, a step at a time.

Shakespeare's plays were popular and widely known during his lifetime. People from different backgrounds all went to the theater. Now, four centuries later, they are no less popular. Shakespeare in the theater, according to the *New York Times,* continues to be a multimillion-dollar enterprise. Yet, though the truths of the human heart have not changed since Shakespeare wrote, the times have changed: His language sounds striking, but is sometimes difficult to understand; some of the ideas he took for granted—the king's holy power to rule, for example, we no longer believe, and the theater for which he wrote, long since burned to the ground, was far different from our theaters, especially from the theater we call television.

First, some ground rules. Shakespeare wrote plays for an audience that knew the story before the play started. If he thought they might not know, as in *Romeo and Juliet,* he had an actor come out and tell them how the play ended. So, to do justice to the television performance of *Richard II,* you should not only know the story, but you should also know the play by reading it carefully; by reading the Pelican introduction, if that is the edition of the play you are using; and, as I will suggest, by trying to get "inside" the play through some experiments in staging. These preparations are best thought of as phases in which, as do theater people, you move from a basic understanding of what the play is about to an exploration of its mysteries and meanings. If you prepare in this way, you will find the television performance richer, more enjoyable, and more meaningful than if you wait to read the play and the commentaries until after you've seen it on television. Put the horse before the cart.

READING *RICHARD II*

Of course there is no single "right" way to read Shakespeare. Some people like to read a little at a time, checking all the footnotes, and stretching it out. Others like to read straight through, looking at the notes only when they are puzzled by a word or an expression. What is essential is that you remember that reading any play, and especially Shakespeare's plays, requires a special kind of imagination and concentration. I would suggest that you start slowly, a scene at a time. Then, to get the full sweep and flow of *Richard II,* reread it more rapidly. It is part of the richness of Shakespeare that each reading, each performance, will reveal new discoveries. These discoveries are one of the pleasures of studying Shakespeare, and students who miss them because they are in a hurry cheat themselves. If a particular passage seems especially good (or, for that matter, especially difficult), read it aloud for the sound and sense of the poetry, which actors say you can almost taste in the big speeches. Now, READ THE PLAY. (If you should become confused, refer to the synopsis.)

After your first reading, but before your second, you should pause, collect your thoughts, and consult others' opinions. Here's how.

MAKE A SCENE PLOT (A LIST OF THE ACTION, TIME, AND PLACE OF EACH SCENE)

Go through the play act-by-act and scene-by-scene, and give each scene a name that defines its main action. You could call III, iv, "The Gardening Scene," for instance, or you could call IV, i, "The Deposing Scene." Having done this, write the numbers of the scenes down the left-hand margin of a sheet of paper, and next to each scene write the name you've given it. Then, going back to the play, look through each scene for a clue to its time and place. Sometimes the editor gives the location at the beginning of the scene. Sometimes Shakespeare does. Sometimes location and time are only implied in what people say. Sometimes Shakespeare doesn't say when and where a scene happens. If he does, it's important (and if he *doesn't,* it's sometimes important too). Your entries for III, iv and IV, i might look something like this:

Act and Scene	Name	Time	Place
III, iv	Gardening Scene	Daytime, summer	A garden outside London
IV, i	Deposing Scene	Shortly afterwards	Westminster Hall (Parliament) in London

Making a list like this (sometimes called a "scene plot") gives a director a handle on the play's shape. Like a road map, it lets you see the whole play at a glance. For students, it is especially useful, because, if you read carefully, you will begin to see that, even though Shakespeare has very few explicit stage directions, he tells what we need to know about time, place, and stage actions through what people say. We can guess that it's broad daylight in the Gardening Scene from the Queen's saying they'll step into "the shadow of these trees" and we can guess it's summertime from the Gardeners' talk about propping up the apricot trees and about the need for weeding—both summertime chores.

When your scene plot is complete, you will have a good idea of how the play moves—its main actions, their unfolding in time and space. To better understand its geographical movement, look at the map of England (Fig. 2) and trace the movements of Richard, Bolingbroke, and the others. To Shakespeare's people and to English people today, there was a solid familiarity about those places, much as if, in an American movie or play, the action moved around the United States from, say, New York to Chicago, Los Angeles, San Francisco, Houston, and then to Washington, D.C. Why does Shakespeare move the action around like this? Part of the answer, of course, is that that's how things happened in history. But Shakespeare didn't worry much about changing or skipping historical details to suit his play. What other reasons are there? Notice that it gives a sense of the entire country being involved in the play, a sense that is underlined by the reference to characters by their titles: Northumberland, York, Gloucester, and so on are all real places, large chunks of the country, as you can see from the map.

Look down your list of the times—time of day and time of year are usually more important to Shakespeare than the actual historical date. Can you see how the play moves from day to day, from season to season, from outdoors to indoors? These movements too give the play a rhythm for the actors and audience that enables Shakespeare to telescope the real "historical" time spanning several years into a couple of hours without wearing out his audience or making them feel hurried. Can you explain why the time for some scenes is more exact than for others?

READ INTRODUCTORY MATERIAL

Now, with the shape and movement of the play well understood, you will want to hear what the scholar Matthew Black, in the Introduction to the Pelican edition, has to say about the play. (If you are not using the Pelican edition of the play, I suggest that you read one or more of the selections listed in the Annotated Bibliography.) If you haven't completed phases 1 and 2, STOP! NEVER READ ANYTHING *ABOUT* THE PLAY BEFORE YOU

Figure 2. Historical map of England and France

READ THE PLAY!!! Students are often too humble or too unsure of themselves to tackle the play itself. While it is true that some help is needed (which is why you're taking this course) that help can count only after you have actually read and begun to think about the play.

Of course, you will not agree with everything Black or any other scholar says, for even the best scholars don't agree with each other about *Richard II*. Beneath their differing viewpoints are two ideas of the play: one as poetry that happens to be a play, the other as a play that happens to be poetry. *Richard II* is one of Shakespeare's early plays, and its poetic language seems much further from "normal" everyday speech than the poetry of his later plays. Of course Shakespeare was often deliberately trying to make the King and Nobles sound elevated. But he was also creating a distance between what people are saying and what they are thinking and feeling behind the formal speeches. In the first scene, for instance, we hear the King, Mowbray, and Bolingbroke all speaking formally and fervently. Justice will be done, they all proclaim. Yet we learn in the next scene from Gaunt that the King himself ordered Gloucester's murder, and that he's trying to cover it up. Throughout the play, we are aware of people speaking what they think will conceal their real thoughts. To distinguish between what's being said and what's being felt, theater people often talk about "text" (what is said) and "subtext" (what is felt). In the big formal scenes, a great deal of the real drama occurs in the tension between text and subtext, between the formal poetry and the cunning, blood-thirsty plots it conceals. If you can start to feel the people behind the poetry, you will have come much closer to the play's center of power in the theater than if you hear only the beautiful words.

Where Shakespeare's audience was tuned in from the start, we today need to develop a sense of the "hidden" drama—or subtext. The opening tournament, his audience knew, could not be played out according to the rules of chivalry because Richard himself had given the orders for murder. Like Richard Nixon asking Haldeman to investigate, Richard II turns to Mowbray for the answer to Gloucester's murder. Richard finally has no choice but to banish the man who helped him commit the crime, in hopes that by banishing both accused and accuser he can cover it up. Behind the pomp and pageantry moves a struggle for power that will eventually unseat Richard. We should watch and listen keenly for signs of it. In the scene with Gaunt the surface of the scene shows the arrogant King taking a poor old man's possessions. Yet we can guess, as Bolingbroke did, that Richard knows of his danger and is trying to keep his rival Bolingbroke weak by seizing his estate, even as he tries to better his own standing by leading the country against a foreign enemy. In the public confrontations between Richard and Bolingbroke at Flint Castle and at the deposition, Richard begins to step out from behind his public personality to reveal his inner suffering, even as Bolingbroke develops his own public personality, using it to deal with Aumerle and the other traitors at the play's end. Beneath the public ceremonies lies a hidden personal dimension, and this, as much as the pageantry, the breaking of the mirror, or Richard's murder, must seize our imaginations.

REREADING *RICHARD II*

Having read the play and the opinions of others, you will now want to reread it, this time trying to move at the pace envisioned by Shakespeare. Don't skip this step. Pick two or three hours when you're at your best, free from distractions from the phone, work, friends, and family. Read the play straight through. As you do, try to *see* it and to *hear* it: the actors coming onstage, greeting each other, shouting challenges, standing, sitting, kneeling, looking now at one character, now at another, and now—for a soliloquy—perhaps at the audience. One of the best ways to complete this phase of your preparation is to read the play while listening to it on records or on tapes. Many public libraries, high schools, and colleges have such recordings, and it would be well worth a phone call or two for you to arrange to hear a recording of *Richard II*. You can also order the records from a record dealer, if you allow enough time. As you reread the play, trying to stage it in your mind, you will have reached the point where most rehearsals begin: The cast of actors gather together with the director and they read through the play aloud, each actor reading his or her part, and the assistant stage manager usually timing each act. While you don't need to worry about the exact time this second reading takes, you should try to make the whole experience of the play fall within its natural length onstage of two to three hours.

AN EXPERIMENT IN STAGING: THE DEPOSITION SCENE

You are now ready to begin to explore the play actively. First, remember that this is *not* a course in theater production; it is a course in Shakespeare, and you should not be afraid to do things that are new to you, or that might look amateur, but that will help take you "inside" *Richard II*. Remember too, that there is no one *right* or *best* way to stage the play. Shakespeare probably wrote more than one version of *Richard II,* and he made it by reshaping the stories he read in history books—half facts and half legend—maybe even borrowing ideas from an earlier play. Since then, stage history shows, the play has been revised, reshaped, and restaged in many different ways, as new audiences come to see new actors perform it. The television production is but the most recent in a long line of "new" *Richard IIs*.

To get into the play, let's try some staging ourselves. The scene I have chosen to try is the Deposition Scene (IV, i), a big scene, and a challenge to any director and actors. Before trying to work with the actors, we need to make some basic decisions about the scene, script, casting, costumes, props, and stage.

To discover how Shakespeare's script helps the director and actors stage the Deposition Scene, we need to think about the scene and the play as a director would. Over four hundred years ago Shakespeare wrote for a theater and an audience quite different from our theaters and audiences today, especially from television and television audiences. On Shakespeare's bare stage before an Elizabethan audience the splendor of medieval pageantry and the ringing sound of the herald's voice stirred emotions then as they do not now. David Giles, the director of the television production of *Richard II*, confessed that the tournament that opens the play had especially perplexed him.[1] How can its stylized ritual be conveyed through the "ultrarealism" (his word) of television? If you go for the ritual, in keeping with the poetry, audiences accustomed to realism may find the tournament only silly. "Where are the horses?" they may ask. Yet if one is wholly realistic, the long soliloquies and the highly wrought poetry may seem artificial. The trick is to strike a balance, so that, like the songs and dances of a musical, the poetry and the ritual fit in with the overall design.

The Scene

Like the tournament that opens the play, the Deposition Scene is another point in the play where Shakespeare insists on ritual. Only a coronation could possibly be more formal and ceremonious than the dethroning of the King before the assembled English nobles and Parliament. The scene has several parts. In the first part (lines 1–106), the nobles assemble: Bagot and Aumerle accuse each other of treason, and the other nobles take sides, one-by-one striding forward to throw down their gages (ceremonial gloves) on the ground in front of Bolingbroke, who presides. Shakespeare's reasons for beginning the scene this way are clear: It separates the supporters of Bolingbroke from those of the King; it sets the serious, ceremonial tone of the occasion; and it prepares for the last parts of the scene where the ceremony, like the mirror, is shattered. In the next part (lines 107–320), comes the actual dethroning. Richard is first brought in to proclaim his crimes and to renounce the throne. He refuses to play his part meekly. Instead he takes command and forces Bolingbroke to seize the crown from him. Then, as he examines his face in the mirror, he reveals his wrenching loss of identity, literally stealing the scene and the audience's sympathy from Bolingbroke. In the last part (lines 321–334), at the very end of the scene, we see that the deposition has already provoked a counterplot against Bolingbroke by the clergy.

The Script

Having sketched out the scene, we must consider the text as a script for staging. If we were to look for a moment over the shoulder of television director Giles, we would see that he cut the scene by about one-third. Beginning with York's entry (line 107), he omitted the first part of the scene (1–106) and then trimmed out Bolingbroke's arrest order (158–61), which doesn't make sense without the opening part of the scene. He also shortened the last part of the scene by cutting the Abbot's closing speech (326–34). Why? Although Giles doesn't say, we can guess that he discarded the ceremony of the gages because it posed special problems for a television audience unfamiliar with the ceremony. And it is not absolutely essential to the main business of the scene—Richard's deposition. Instead of the ceremony of the gages, to establish the ritual occasion, he relied on television's ability to show much of the Westminster setting that Shakespeare's audience had to imagine.

Is such "tampering" with Shakespeare's text justified? Many scholars would argue that it is not; many theater people, that it is essential if the play is to be effective with a modern audience. Of course, the question can never be resolved in absolute terms. For this experiment, however, let us accept David Giles's judgment, and begin our staging where he began his. Mark the cuts in your text and proceed.

Casting and Characterization

When Shakespeare wrote his plays, he wrote with particular actors in mind (no actresses, as young boys played the women's parts). Directors today try to match the actors who are available with the parts as they conceive them. Casting is perhaps the single most important step in putting on the play. First, what roles are needed for the Deposition Scene. Who is onstage? Essentially, there are two groups: Bolingbroke's men (Northumberland, York, Fitzwater, Bagot, Another Lord, Heralds, and Officers) and Richard's, led by Aumerle (Surrey, Percy, Bishop Carlisle, and the Abbot of Westminster). How will we cast the scene? Everyone who has worked in the theater knows that most casting is type-casting. Say you want to bring out a contrast between Bolingbroke the man of action and Richard the idle dreamer (but one of many possibilities, for Bolingbroke can be seen as a schemer, and Richard as a martyr misguided by bad advisors). Then your Bolingbroke must be physically impressive and robust; your Richard, perhaps slender and slow to move. Good actors will bring out the facets of their own personalities that suit the role. I remember, for instance when in 1973 the Royal Shakespeare Company staged the play with Ian Richardson (short, wiry, brisk) and Richard Pasco (tall, dignified, poetic) alternating in the two roles, switching from one night to the next. What emerged were two different Richards, two different Bolingbrokes.

Supposing for a moment that we can pick the best actors, what kinds of people, with what personalities and physical traits does the play require? Go back through the play and look carefully, noting everything that's said by or about individual characters that might give clues to their personality or appearance. Shakespeare's text is wonderfully rich and suggestive, sometimes so suggestive that it contains contradictions in it that one cannot resolve. Follow your best impressions and prepare a list of characters with notes on each. Use a separate sheet of paper for each of the major characters. To help you get started, I have begun the list below. For minor characters, a phrase or a sentence is enough; the major parts require more.

Bolingbroke. Strong, virile, physically active. Without insisting on his exact age, he should seem to be in his late thirties, roughly the same age as Richard. He is the kind of man who can speak well, but who knows (as at Flint Castle) the power of silence. In this scene a new costume would help to set him off from his earlier self: He has won, and he should look ready for victory and the crown. For him the power of kingship to do good or evil outweighs the sacred nature of the office. He opposes Richard because he is a bad ruler, not because he killed Gloucester, although that is given as an ostensible reason. In this scene Richard embarasses and upstages him.

Northumberland. (Age: vigorous mid-fifties). A tall, tough outdoorsman (he lives in rough country and doesn't seem to mind marching around all over England, nor does he show sympathy for Richard's soft living or pity for his weakness). A soldier, loyal in his way, but first of all looking out for his own good. A man of power, he respects power, not ideas or morality. People don't really trust him, he knows it, and he doesn't care. He lives in his armor, with his sword at his side. No time for women. No patience with weakness. But no leader. A maker and unmaker of kings, but no king himself.

In this scene, he's determined to get Richard out of the way, and to do this, he wants a public confession: Richard must read the list of his crimes, no matter how hard it is for him to do it. When Northumberland arrests Carlisle we see how he works: Like an attack dog, he springs forward as soon as Carlisle finishes. Query: Does Bolingbroke signal him to get Carlisle? Or does he do it on his own? If Bolingbroke does signal (a nod of the head?) when does it come? When Carlisle calls Bolingbroke (Hereford) traitor? Northumberland's insistence that Richard read the papers contrasts with Bolingbroke's milder (and wiser) realization that Richard is winning points with his eloquent speeches, and that, if he's humored, he'll hand the crown over in the end anyway.

As you work on these character notes, draw on your knowledge of people as well as on the clues Shakespeare gives you. This is how an actor creates a role, and it is an exciting process. There are clues everywhere. Nothing says Northumberland is tall, for example, but it's hinted at when Richard calls him a "ladder" by which Bolingbroke ascends the throne (V, i). At this point you should start to feel as if you "know" the characters. Even if you're not certain at every moment just what they're thinking, you should be able to make shrewd guesses as to what they *might* be thinking.

Costumes

As you study the text for clues to character, you will see that Shakespeare provides some hints for costumes. Sometimes he is explicit—York needs to put on his boots in V, ii, for instance. Sometimes he is less so, leaving it to our common sense to assume that soldiers will be in battle gear, that the King and court will be in special attire, that the Gardeners look like gardeners, and so on. How does one realize Shakespeare's intentions, when they can be discovered? This is the designer's art. To give our exercise point and focus, go back to your list of character sketches and add some costume notes.

In Shakespeare's theater, we know that actors wore contemporary dress. Not everyday clothes, necessarily, for the actors playing nobles often were dressed in hand-me-downs from real nobles, and these clothes were lavish and colorful. Yet they usually did not try to dress in costumes appropriate to the time of the play's action: no togas for Rome, no kilts for Scotland, and no medieval outfits for *Richard II*. Of course we are more accustomed to "period dress"—costumes appropriate to the times. And for us, it would only be silly to dress a medieval history play in modern clothes. Or the clothes could be timeless: robes, tunics, trousers of no particular period. Choose a time period (or none) and explain why you think that's best (write it down). What colors should be used? How many are needed? How can the costumes show the characters' personalities? Strong colors (white, red, blue, black, yellow) are often used to distinguish the main characters one from another, and plainer colors (dark brown, green, grey), for less important characters.

Now, imagine that you are standing in the wings waiting for the last dress rehearsal of the scene to be called. The actors stand there silently, some smiling quietly at each other, some only looking off into space as the weeping Queen reproves the Gardeners, and they reply in gruff country accents. What will these actors look like? At one entrance stand York and Richard; at the other, the assembled nobles, with the herald ready to enter first, and Bolingbroke at the end of the line.

Upon your imaginary forces work! The Chorus's exhortation from *Henry V* resounds: "And eke out our performance with your mind" (III, Cho., 35). Bring each actor out into the light and describe what you see. Let the costumes and physical appearance reflect not only the requirements of the text, but also your own sense of the character, as sketched in your notes. To get things started, I have made costume notes for Bolingbroke and Northumberland, a list of the others follows. Copy it and make your costume notes on separate sheets of paper.

Bolingbroke. In a moment Bolingbroke expects to ascend the throne. Whenever we saw him earlier, he was in armor, now he wears his court robes, broad bands of crimson trim on a white cape, with a darker, blue-black doublet underneath. Usually an active man, full of motion onstage, in this scene he is constrained by the ceremony. He conveys his alert responses through his eyes, looking the situation over and sizing things up. His other movements should seem to be decorous, even regal. We must sense the quick mind that can respond without loss of balance to Carlisle's and Richard's eloquent threats.

Northumberland. This harsh and clever man expects to be the power behind the throne, not ruling the country himself, but making sure that the ruler protects his interests in Northumberland. His long black cloak is trimmed with silver embroidery, as is his doublet. He too keeps his eye on everything, taking his cue to action from Bolingbroke. His greatest shortcoming is that he's too ruthless: he doesn't know when to stop insisting that Richard read over his crimes. For this reason, he could never rule except as a tyrant.

There's a start. Now continue for the other characters:

Aumerle	Attendant 2
Percy	Attendant 3
Fitzwater	Herald
Surrey	Bagot
Another Lord	Duke of York
Bishop of Carlisle	King Richard II
Abbot of Westminster	Officer 1
Attendant 1 (gets mirror)	Officer 2

Props

The script calls for several props in this scene. These are small, portable things needed for the action, and they might include also items of costume that are signs of office: The Bishop and Abbot would have something that indicated their offices, the King has crown and sceptre, the Officers and Noblemen would have gages (less important, as we are beginning at line 107) and swords. Besides these, there are other essential props, which you can discover by carefully reading the scene. Without them, the scene wouldn't work. To these essentials, you may wish to add others: a flag for Bolingbroke, banners for the Attendants 1 and 2, and so on. For everything you do, you should have good reasons, ideas that come from the actual words of the play.

PROP LIST

Essential
9 pairs of gages (gloves)
9 nobles' swords (rapiers)
1 bishop's medal on chain
1 bishop's official hat
1 abbot's medal
1 abbot's hat
1 mirror

Others
1 flag
2 banners

I have begun the prop list, and I ask you to complete it.

Staging

Our actors assembled, the play well in hand, and the costumes and props prepared, we are now ready to try some staging, moving the actors and making the last scene come to life. What shall we do for a stage? As Lord Bardolph says, "when we mean to build/We first survey the plot, then we draw the model" (I, iii, 41–42). And so we shall. The materials needed can be as simple or as fancy as you like, but you will need a pencil, an eraser, some sheets of paper, and something to stand for the actors. You can make actors out of colored pipe cleaners if you like, or even use different coins, buttons, or bottle tops. I will begin the exercise, but it will be up to you to finish it on your own. The Deposition Scene is a "big" scene, a challenge to any director and actors. Before trying to move the actors, we need to make some basic decisions about stage and scenery.

As far as we can tell, Shakespeare's actors worked in a theater that looked essentially like that shown in Figure 3. It was a large platform, roughly the size of a singles tennis court (one side of the net). It stuck out from the back wall, in which there were two (perhaps three) doors. On three sides the audience stood (near the stage) or sat (in galleries surrounding the stage). Above the stage, supported by two pillars was some kind of balcony, which was probably used for Flint Castle in the original staging of *Richard II*. In this theater, plays were put on in the afternoons, using natural light. One scene followed another without a break (there was no curtain nor, of course, any blackouts). The ground plan looked something like the one in Figure 4.

Although we are accustomed to scenery in our theaters, it can be very useful to see how Shakespeare achieved his effects without it, which you can do if you use this ground plan. Enlarge it so that it's big enough to hold your "actors" comfortably: it only takes a pot lid and a ruler. You also might want to copy the perspective sketch of the theater, making several copies, so that you can sketch in what the scene looks like from one big moment to the next.

Figure 3. In this modified sketch of an Elizabethan public playhouse, it can be seen that a neutral stage extends well into the ground, or yard, where much of the audience stood to watch the action on the stage. Higher-paying customers occupied sheltered boxes around the sides. Most of the theater is open to the sky.

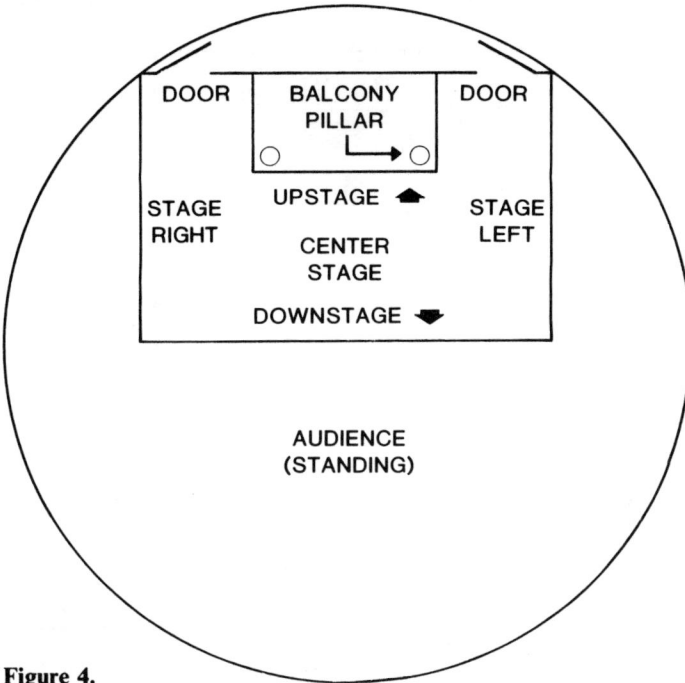

Figure 4.

These are necessary steps to help you visualize the scene. Designers in the theater regularly do this (the sketches are sometimes called "story boards"), and they help to get the play up on its feet.

Blocking: The Promptscript. Now you're ready to "move" the scene, to direct the movements and actions of the actors. Get out the pipe cleaners, buttons, or whatever. Using the enlarged ground plan, gather your actors (each identified by color, or by an initial written on a piece of adhesive tape and stuck on the figure). Make an extra copy of the scene or use your text and some extra blank pages, so that you can mark down what you want the actors to do, as you move them onstage. To suggest how this might be done, I have made a sample promptscript and a stage map showing three movements for the first half of the scene (see Fig. 5 a, b, c).

As you can see, something is needed to replace the ceremony of the gages that sets the tone at the beginning of the scene. The business with the banners and the fanfare for the procession is meant to accomplish the same thing. The nobles form into groups: those for and those against Bolingbroke (which might be enhanced by dressing Bolingbroke's supporters in colors like his—black, red, white—and Richard's in contrasting colors—such as brown, green, and ocher). The throne behind Bolingbroke is almost a character itself, for it polarizes the stage and it keeps drawing Bolingbroke to it, and with him the

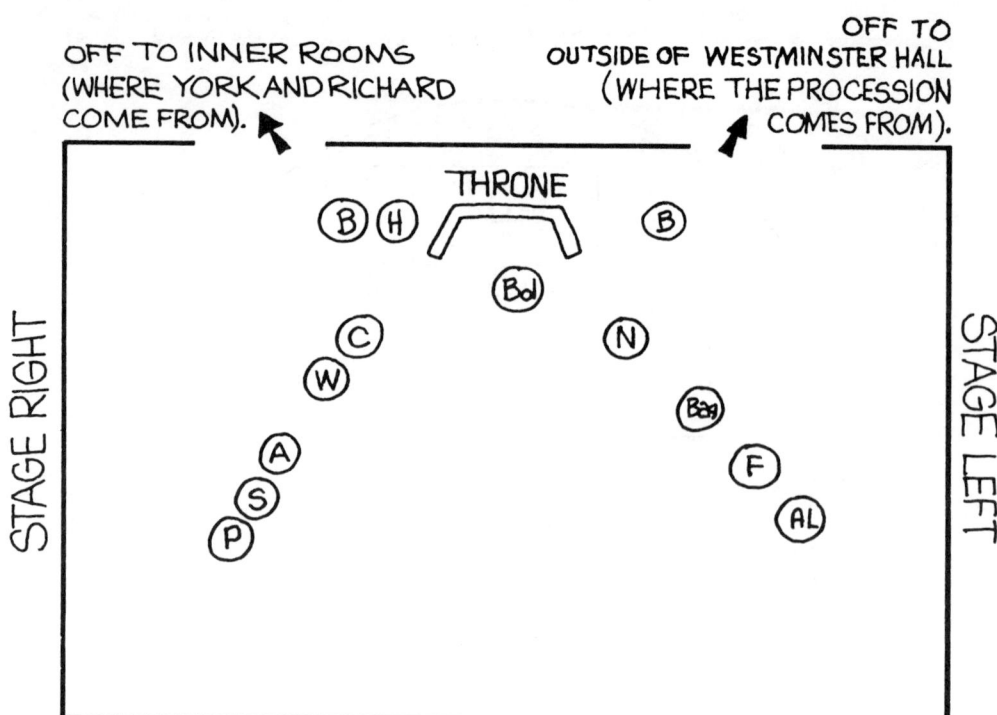

- B = BANNER
- H = HERALD
- Bol = BOLINGBROKE
- N = NORTHUMBERLAND
- Bag = BAGOT
- F = FITZWATER
- AL = ANOTHER LORD
- C = CARLISLE
- W = ABBOT OF WESTMINSTER
- A = AUMERLE
- S = SURREY
- P = PERCY

Figure 5A.

Figure 5A. *Continued*

WESTMINSTER HALL

BEFORE SCENE BEGINS, 2 PAGES ENTER AND SET THRONE ONSTAGE.

THROUGHOUT THE SCENE, STAGE LEFT DOOR LEADS OUTSIDE (WHERE BOLINGBROKE COMES FROM) AND STAGE RIGHT LEADS INSIDE (WHERE RICHARD AND YORK COME FROM). ENTER FIRST TWO OFFICERS WITH BANNERS WHO TAKE THEIR POSITIONS. THEN A TRUMPET FANFARE (OFFSTAGE) BEGINS AND CONTINUES UNTIL ALL ARE ON. THEN THE HEARLD ENTERS LEADING THE PROCESSION. THEY MARCH SOLEMNLY, TAKING THEIR

Enter Bolingbroke, with the Lords [Aumerle, Northumberland, Percy, Fitzwater, Surrey, and another, with Bishop of Carlisle, Abbot of Westminster, Attendants, and Herald] to Parliament.   IV, i

PLACES AS SHOWN ON THE STAGE MAP. ORDER OF ENTRANCE: PERCY, ANOTHER LORD, BAGOT, FITZWATER, SURRY, BISHOP OF CARLISLE, ABBOT OF WESTMINSTER, THEN NORTHUMBERLAND, AND BOLINGBROKE LAST.

THE EXACT ORDER OF THE PROCESSION IS NOT AS IMPORTANT AS ITS SOLEMNITY. THE ORDER IS ROUGHLY FROM LEAST IMPORTANT TO THE CLERGY TO BOLINGBROKE.

44 The Tragedy of King Richard the Second

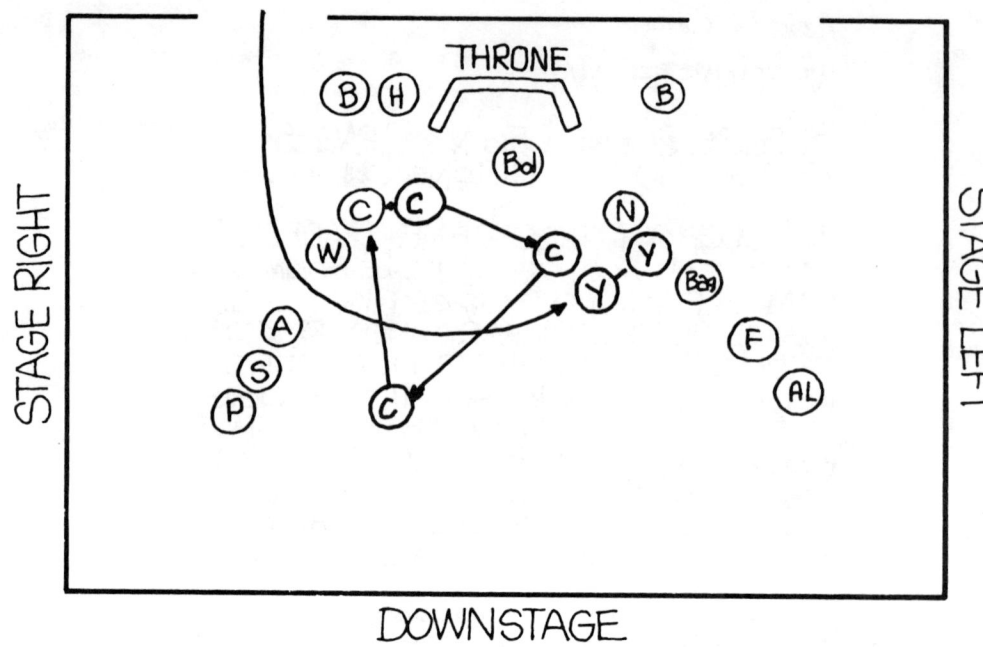

Ⓨ = YORK

Figure 5B.

Figure 5B. *Continued*

YORK ENTERS AS THE FANFARE STOPS. HE COMES TO BOLINGBROKE AND DROPS TO ONE KNEE, THEN SPEAKS.	——— *Enter York [attended].*
	YORK
	  Great Duke of Lancaster, I come to thee
	  From plume-plucked Richard, who with willing soul
	  Adopts thee heir and his high sceptre yields
	  To the possession of thy royal hand.
	  Ascend his throne, descending now from him,
	  And long live Henry, fourth of that name!
	BOLINGBROKE
	  In God's name I'll ascend the regal throne.———
		THROUGH OUT THE NOBLES EXCHANGE NERVOUS GLANCES. THE ABBOT NODS IN SUPPORT OF CARLISLE FROM TIME TO TIME.

CARLISLE'S OUT BURST STOPS YORK.
 	
CARLISLE TAKES A STEP FORWARD AS IF TO STOP BOLINGBROKE PHYSICALLY.
 	
DURING SPEECH CARLISLE MOVES THAT HE SPEAKS TO EACH IN TURN (SEE MAP).
	CARLISLE
	  Marry, God forbid!
	  Worst in this royal presence may I speak,
	  Yet, best beseeming me to speak the truth:
	  Would God that any in this noble presence
	  Were enough noble to be upright judge
	  Of noble Richard! then true noblesse would
	  Learn him forbearance from so foul a wrong.
	  What subject can give sentence on his king?
	  And who sits here that is not Richard's subject?
	  Thieves are not judged but they are by to hear,
	  Although apparent guilt be seen in them;
	  And shall the figure of God's majesty,
	  His captain, steward, deputy elect,
	  Anointed, crownèd, planted many years,
	  Be judged by subject and inferior breath,
	  And he himself not present? O, forfend it God
	  That, in a Christian climate, souls refined
	  Should show so heinous, black, obscene a deed!
		YORK RISES, STEPS ASIDE. HE PROCLAIMS IN A LOUD VOICE, AND TURNS AS IF TO STEP TO THE THRONE.
		
		STANDS (NOT SITS)
		
		LOOKS UP

LOOKS AROUND AT THEM ALL.	I speak to subjects, and a subject speaks,
	  Stirred up by God, thus boldly for his king.
	  My Lord of Hereford here, whom you call king,
	  Is a foul traitor to proud Hereford's king;
	  And if you crown him, let me prophesy,
	  The blood of English shall manure the ground
	  And future ages groan for this foul act;
	  Peace shall go sleep with Turks and infidels,
	  And in this seat of peace tumultuous wars
	  Shall kin with kin and kind with kind confound;
	  Disorder, horror, fear, and mutiny
	  Shall here inhabit, and this land be called
	  The field of Golgotha and dead men's skulls.
		BOLINGBROKE AND NORTHUMBERLAND EXCHANGE GLANCES. BOLINGBROKE RESTRAINS NORTHUMBERLAND, WHO SEEMS READY TO SPRING FORWARD.

CARLISLE ENDS SPEECH WITH A SWEEPING GESTURE THAT ENDS WITH HIM POINTING.	O, if you raise this house against this house,
	  It will the woefullest division prove
	  That ever fell upon this cursèd earth.
	  Prevent it, resist it, let it not be so,
	  Lest child, child's children cry against you woe.	

46 The Tragedy of King Richard the Second

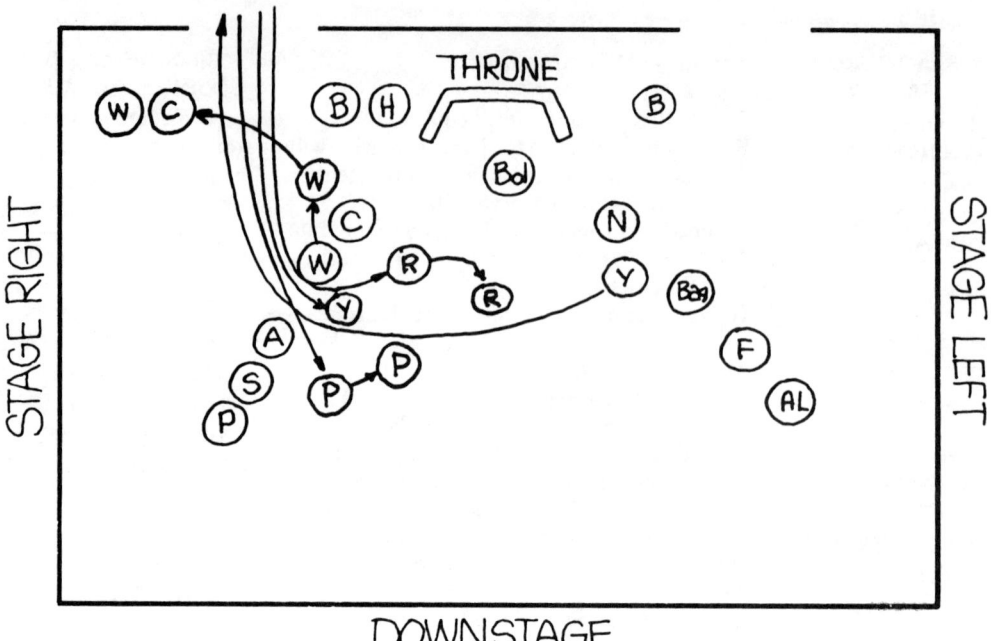

Ⓟ = PAGE
Ⓡ = RICHARD

Figure 5C.

Figure 5C. *Continued*

WESTMINSTER STEPS FORWARD BEHIND CARLISLE

TO FILL IN THE TIME, WESTMINSTER TAKES CARLISLE STAGE RIGHT. BOLINGBROKE STEPS BACK TO THRONE AND STANDS ON ITS FIRST STEP.

LOOKS AROUND

SHOUTS IT OUT
PAUSES.
THE SILENCE IS DEAFENING

RICHARD TURNS SO THAT HE STANDS CENTER STAGE, HIS BACK TO BOLINGBROKE, THE CROWN HELD OUT TO STAGE LEFT. HE SPEAKS TO THE AUDIENCE AS IF TO PARLIAMENT.

NORTHUMBERLAND
Well have you argued, sir; and for your pains
Of capital treason we arrest you here.
My Lord of Westminster, be it your charge
To keep him safely till his day of trial.
[May it please you, lords, to grant the commons' suit.
BOLINGBROKE
Fetch hither Richard, that in common view
He may surrender. So we shall proceed
Without suspicion.
YORK   I will be his conduct.   *Exit.*

Enter Richard and York [with Officers bearing the crown, &c.]. Page
RICHARD
Alack, why am I sent for to a king
Before I have shook off the regal thoughts
Wherewith I reigned? I hardly yet have learned
To insinuate, flatter, bow, and bend my limbs.
Give sorrow leave a while to tutor me
To this submission. Yet I well remember
The favors of these men. Were they not mine?
Did they not sometime cry 'All hail!' to me?
So Judas did to Christ; but he, in twelve,
Found truth in all but one; I, in twelve thousand none.
God save the king! Will no man say amen?
Am I both priest and clerk? Well then, amen!
God save the king! although I be not he;
And yet amen, if heaven do think him me.
To do what service am I sent for hither?
YORK
To do that office of thine own good will
Which tired majesty did make thee offer –
The resignation of thy state and crown
To Henry Bolingbroke.
RICHARD
Give me the crown. Here, cousin, seize the crown.
Here, cousin,
On this side my hand, and on that side yours.
Now is this golden crown like a deep well
That owes two buckets, filling one another,
The emptier ever dancing in the air,
The other down, unseen, and full of water.
That bucket down and full of tears am I,
Drinking my griefs whilst you mount up on high.
BOLINGBROKE
I thought you had been willing to resign.
RICHARD
My crown I am, but still my griefs are mine.
You may my glories and my state depose,
But not my griefs. Still am I king of those.
BOLINGBROKE
Part of your cares you give me with your crown.
RICHARD
Your cares set up do not pluck my cares down.
My care is loss of care, by old care done;
Your care is gain of care, by new care won.
The cares I give I have, though given away;
They tend the crown, yet still with me they stay.
BOLINGBROKE
Are you contented to resign the crown?

AS IF ON CUE FROM BOLINGBROKE, NORTHUMBERLAND SPEAKS, LOOKING AT THE OTHERS AS HE DOES. ON "TREASON" THERE IS A BIG REACTION FROM THE OTHERS.

YORK BUSTLES IN. THE PAGE HAS CROWN AND SCEPTRE ON A CUSHION. HE STANDS MUTE

PAGE STEPS FORWARD. RICHARD TAKES THE CROWN, HOLDS IT OUT TO BOLINGBROKE IN A BIG GESTURE BUT DOES NOT GO TO HIM. BOLINGBROKE HOLDS HIS GROUND. NORTHUMBERLAND LOOKS AROUND ANXIOUSLY. THE OTHERS ARE FROZEN EXCEPT FOR THE TWO CLERGYMEN, WHO WHISPER TO EACH OTHER.

attention of the others. York, whom I imagine as a good-hearted, avuncular bumbler, sets off two dramatic explosions that ruin the planned deposition. First he all-hails Bolingbroke *before* Richard has confessed, thereby releasing Carlisle's righteous indignation, and undermining the effective transfer of power. He preaches to the audience and to each of the nobles as he does his circular movement. Northumberland, heavy-handed as always, puts him under arrest (only after getting the nod from Bolingbroke). For his part, Bolingbroke keeps his eye on the main chance—the crown—and lets Carlisle and Richard have their say. Westminster of course is the last one to be charged with enforcing Carlisle's arrest, and when he draws him aside (to make stage room for Richard, York, and the Page) we may imagine that the two clerics whisper about the plot they open out at the end of the scene. The other, silent nobles must set the anxious, uncertain tone of the scene by their reactions and by their frozen postures.

It's the kind of occasion when anything might happen, and the stakes are the highest: a kingdom and the king's power of life and death over his subjects. When Richard does enter, there must be a big reaction, almost as if people went to kneel by reflex and then stopped themselves. Richard sees it, and takes over. By having Bolingbroke on the first step of the throne, we can have Richard downstage of him without blocking him from view, and the arrangement gives Richard full scope for his scene stealing, with the audience onstage and in the theater. By this staging, the audience is, in effect, taking the place of Parliament, the representatives of the people, and the actors should play the scene as if they are taking part in a public ceremony gone awry.

Experiment with different stagings until you find one that seems best. It should first of all respond with movement and gesture to what the text requires. For clarity, those speaking should be easily seen by the audience. Downstage, the position nearest the audience, is usually the "strongest" position, and this is where the main actor wants to be when he gets to the scene's climax. What is the climax toward which the scene builds—the most intense moment? Is it when Richard shatters the mirror? Or is it afterward, when Richard speaks to Bolingbroke:

> *Mark, silent king, the moral of this sport—*
> *How soon my sorrow hath destroyed my face.*

(IV, i, 290–91)

Does Richard move toward Bolingbroke? Or Bolingbroke to him? Or do they only stand silent before Bolingbroke replies—with concern? With disdain? With sorrow? With a smile?

> *The shadow of your sorrow hath destroyed*
> *The shadow of your face.*

(IV, i, 292–93)

Does Bolingbroke speak only to Richard? Or is he speaking to the assembled nobles too, trying to stay on top of the situation? Like the director and actors, you must answer these questions for which there is no one single answer, only possible solutions.

Once you have gotten "inside" the play in this way, you can see that these kinds of questions lead to larger and larger questions: Is the play truly about Richard as a bad king, making it a history play that shows how *not* to rule a country? Or is it about Richard the would-be king, a victim of Bolingbroke the crafty politician? If we take one line or the other, we want to build sympathy for either Bolingbroke or for Richard, not just in this scene, but in others as well. With each moment the actors and director must choose, deciding to go one way, rather than others, and the sum of these decisions is a fresh production of the play. Because each production is new, people return again and again to re-experience the play. In this way, while the television production of *Richard II* may be your first *Richard II*, it should not be your last.

WATCHING *RICHARD II* ON TELEVISION

If you have prepared thoroughly, now you should be ready to enjoy the television production. Because theatergoing is a group experience, you'll enjoy the show even more if you watch the play in the company of friends and family, with whom you can share the results of your preparation. A delightful sense of anticipation runs through the theater before the curtain goes up, just as it should run through your home television audience as the play begins.

Of course Shakespeare didn't write for television, and so the televised *Richard II* offers certain advantages and disadvantages. The small screen makes it hard to give a sense of the pageantry of the crowd scenes that swell the stage. At the same time, close-ups can bring us into strong emotional contact with the actors. You will notice the way director David Giles uses close-ups to enhance sympathy for Derek Jacobi's Richard at the end of the play.

Some people used to bring texts of the play to the theater to follow along, and you still sometimes sit next to someone who seems to have the play memorized, and who keeps whispering to friends about what got left out. A few years ago, in the front row of the Stratford, Ontario, theater, two school teachers were sitting with their book, talking and criticizing as the play went on. The leading actor, without interrupting his speech, did a low, graceful bow to the teachers, snatched the book, and threw it into the wings. The theater exploded in applause. To truly enjoy the play, you must enter into the spirit of the production, allow the actors to take you with them willingly. Put away your books and your cares, and let the play take you away. The time for reflection and criticism comes *after* the play is over, not during it. So sit down, get comfortable, and enjoy the show!

REFLECTIONS

Having seen the play on television, you will now want to consider some of the questions the play raises. Remember that these questions have no final answers. But that has not stopped people from thinking about them for hundreds of years, for it is part of the Shakespeare magic that, just as each staging of the play is new, the play makes us see our own world and our own life with new eyes.

Begin with your preparations. Read over your notes. Were there things that the television *Richard II* did that make you want to change your mind? Take your time, and try to figure out why the actors and director did things differently than you imagined they would. Were the characters as you had imagined them? Could they have been better acted? How? Where do you think the sympathy was meant to fall? Mainly for Richard? Mainly for Bolingbroke? Or a little of both? How do you think director Giles and his actors thought of the play? As a study in power politics? As an illustration of an important chapter in English history? Did you find different parts of the production more satisfying than others? If so, which ones, and why? What got in the way in the slack parts? Can you imagine ways to remedy any shortcomings? How?

Looking beyond the production itself, we can see that the play contains questions that touch our lives today. Although we no longer believe in being ruled by a king who represents God's power on earth—or by any king (that having gone out the window with the Declaration of Independence)—we do believe that in some way the office is greater than the man. Long after President Richard M. Nixon was deemed to have committed a number of crimes, some of the most powerful persons in the country still felt that he should not be removed from office lest the strength of the office be impaired. Shakespeare not only raises the issue of what to do when the ruler abuses (or seems to abuse) his power, he looks beyond to take us into the suffering of a man whose power and physical beauty had made his life so special that he was above other men. He also brings us face to face with the unknowable in politics: how much Bolingbroke is the man of the moment, how much he made those moments. It is impossible to tell. We see too how quickly great power can lead to great crimes, Richard's murder of Gloucester by mere wish being repeated in his own death at the hands of Sir Piers. It is Shakespeare's special gift that he takes us behind the scenes of history so that we can understand it as happening to real people who think and feel as we do. No matter what we may do in life, there are times when we must stand up and speak out for our own—as Bolingbroke does—and we can never tell what the consequences will be. So too, like Gaunt and Bolingbroke, fathers and sons are divided when one considers the needs of the state, the other his own needs. How many times the rift that separates Gaunt and his son Harry split father from son during the Vietnam era! Then too, although Shakespeare touches only lightly on it, there was a persistent legend that Richard had been seduced not only in mind but also in body by the "caterpillars" with whom he played, keeping him from his queen and from the manly exercise of kingship. And here too, we see how great power can lead to great temptation: the neglect of family, and the indulgence of the whims of the moment. No moralist giving an easy lesson, Shakespeare makes us feel the anguish of one who wasted time while still not giving any easy answer as to how, given his high station, he might have behaved otherwise. At the end the question still remains: What are we to do to rule ourselves, in justice, peace, and harmony?

ANNOTATED BIBLIOGRAPHY

Barkan, Leonard. "The Theatrical Consistency of *Richard II.*" *Shakespeare Quarterly* 29 (Winter 1978):5–19.
Barkan defines dramatic action as, in addition to the unfolding of the narrative, a sequence of emotional responses, both among the stage characters and between the characters and the audience. The responses have a certain design, which he calls the play's "emotional consistency"—defined in this instance as texture and logical continuity. Barkan proposes to show that the emotional consistency of *Richard II* concerns passionate or violent energies that are suppressed and built up, then released in both physical violence and comedy. This theory is an interesting one for a play not generally considered violent or comedic.
Brown, John Russell. "Narrative and Focus: *Richard II.*" In his *Shakespeare's Plays in Performance*. Cambridge: Cambridge University Press, 1966.
Brown's essay is a good theatrical commentray and summary. He provides new insight into Richard the play and Richard the character by his suggestions for when, where, and on whom the focus should be and for what the narrative should accomplish at given places in the play.
Gielgud, John. "King Richard the Second." In his *Stage Directions*. London: Heinemann, 1963.
Considered one of the greatest Richards of all time, Gielgud discusses the complexities of the role. Among other things, he notes that the most difficult problem is to achieve and maintain a "straightforward musical rendering of the verse" and still make the action in the play appear spontaneous and convincing.
Rabkin, Norman. *Shakespeare and the Common Understanding,* pp. 80–101. New York: Free Press, 1967.
Rabkin argues that *Richard II* is more than simply a sensitive telling of "a peculiar and local political problem," more than a treatise on the necessity of maintaining Elizabethan ideals and order. He states that the play is a tragedy not so much of systems but of men. Thus our response to the politics of the play is not to the theory within it but rather to the men whose lives and actions create the necessity of theory. The power of the play comes from the many levels of ambivalence Shakespeare creates—questions of the necessity of the continued order of the state versus a king manifestly unfit to rule; the human and emotional but incompetent man/king Richard who excites our sympathies as opposed to the competent but rather unsympathetic usurper, Bolingbroke.

Van Doren, Mark. *"Richard II."* In his *Shakespeare*. Garden City, N.Y.: Doubleday, 1953.

In this essay, Van Doren notes that Shakespeare, very much enthralled with poetry when he wrote *Richard II*, created in the character Richard a great minor poet. Through Richard, Shakespeare expressed his love for language, writing the musical poetry that has never failed to captivate readers.

Note

1. Quoted in an essay on the television production in *The BBC Shakespeare: Richard II* (New York: Mayflower Books, 1978), pp, 19–26. This edition marks the director's cuts in the script, which I have followed.

SELF-TEST

Multiple-choice Questions
1. Shakespeare's Richard possesses a complex personality. ALL BUT ONE of the following descriptions of Richard are appropriate:
    a. He is compassionate, trusting, and blindly loyal to his friends.
    b. He is passive, weak, and indecisive.
    c. He is introspective, imaginative, and eloquent.
    d. He is mercurial, self-conscious, and knowingly dramatic.
    e. He is arrogant, extravagant, and imprudent.
2. He is conservative, cautious, and diplomatic.
    a. Mowbray
    b. Bolingbroke
    c. York
    d. Aumerle
    e. Northumberland
3. He is cynical, powerful, and unsympathetic.
    a. Mowbray
    b. Bolingbroke
    c. York
    d. Aumerle
    e. Northumberland
4. Why does Richard stop the tournament and banish Mowbray and Bolingbroke from England?
    a. to save his cousin, Bolingbroke, from certain death
    b. A tournament was risky; Richard could easily have Bolingbroke killed in exile as he had Gloucester.
    c. to appear unbiased and cover up his own guilt
    d. to force a confession from one of them
    e. He had learned Bolingbroke's followers had rigged the tournament against Mowbray.
5. York tries vainly to persuade Richard not to confiscate Bolingbroke's property with ALL BUT ONE of the following arguments:
    a. The act is unworthy of royalty.
    b. By violating the sacredness of inheritance, Richard is setting a dangerous precedent.
    c. Such an act will turn many loyal subjects against the king.
    d. The act would sully the reputations of his illustrious father (Prince of Wales) and grandfather (Edward III).
    e. If Richard acted against Bolingbroke, York's favorite nephew, York would turn against Richard.
6. Gaunt believes in the divine right of kings. Is this statement part of the explicit text of the play or the implicit subtext?
    a. text
    b. subtext
7. Bolingbroke wants to be king. Is this statement part of the explicit text of the play or the implicit subtext?
    a. text
    b. subtext

8. Bolingbroke, now Henry IV, wanted the death of the deposed Richard. Is this statement part of the explicit text of the play or the implicit subtext?
   a. text
   b. subtext
9. Which of the following quotations is a self-description by the Duke of Lancaster?
   a. "However God or fortune cast my lot,
      There lives or dies, true to Richard's throne,
      A loyal, just, and upright gentleman."
   b. "Within me grief hath kept a tedious fast;
      And who abstains from meat that is not gaunt?"
   c. "In war was never lion raged more fierce,
      In peace was never gentle lamb more mild,
      Than was that young and princely gentleman."
   d. "A brittle glory shineth in this face.
      As brittle as the glory is the face,
      For there it is, cracked in a hundred shivers."
   e. "thus play I in one person many people,
      And none contented."
10. With the murder of Richard, it can be said that Shakespeare brings the play full cycle and right back to its beginning. What would suggest such an interpretation?
    a. The play begins and ends with a banishment.
    b. The play begins and ends with the coronation of a new king.
    c. The play begins and ends with the reigning king being indirectly involved in the murder of a royal relative.
    d. The play begins and ends with Shakespeare's condemnation of good men who become villainous kings.
    e. The play begins and ends with civil law, but now it is Henry IV whose reign is being threatened.

Short-answer Essay Questions

1. Why are the characters referred to by their titles rather than their names; for example, Lancaster, York, Hereford, and Norfolk?
2. Why is *Richard II* written in verse?
3. Discuss the problems that arise for a modern director because Richard's implication in Gloucester's death is not fully revealed until the second scene in Act I.
4. What is the significance of the Garden Scene (III, iv) to the play as a whole?
5. How do the character and personality of Richard II change over the course of the play? What do we know about him, and how is the audience persuaded to feel about him at the beginning of the play and by the end of the play?

Questions for Reflection

1. Do you feel *Richard II* is "poetry that happens to be a play" or a "play that happens to be poetry"? Support your arguments with specific references to the text and to the television production.
2. Find a scene in *Richard II* in which you think the text is at odds with the subtext. Describe the differences between the two. How are these realized in the television production?

3. What kind of man is Richard II? From your character notes write a full description of him. How does your idea of the man compare with that of Derek Jacobi, who plays Richard in the BBC production?
4. Why, in your opinion, does Henry IV pardon Aumerle in the face of clear evidence of his treason and in spite of Aumerle's own father's entreaties to have him punished? Is this decision a strength or a flaw in Henry's character? In the play? Does the treatment of this scene in the television production satisfy you?
5. *Richard II* is a play that can only be understood and appreciated by an audience with an intimate and detailed knowledge of English history. The intrigues and nuances are lost on non-British audiences. Do you agree? Why? Why not?

ANSWER KEY

Answers to Multiple-choice Questions
1. a (evidence throughout play)
2. c (II, i; II, iii)
3. e (III, iii; IV, i)
4. c (I, iii)
5. e (II, i)
6. a (I, iii:
    God's the quarrel; for God's substitute,
    His deputy anointed in his sight,
    Hath caused his death; the which if wrongfully,
    Let heaven revenge; for I may never lift
    An angry arm against his minister.")
7. b (suggested in II, iii)
8. a (V, vi:
    "They love not poison that do poison need,
    Nor do I thee. Though I did wish him dead,
    I hate the murderer, love him murdered.")
9. b (II, i)
10. c (I, i; V, vi)

Suggested Answers to Short-answer Essay Questions
1. These references are to the various geographical regions of England over which the characters so named ruled. English audiences knew these places; thus, the entire country of England, as represented by the nobles of these regions, is seen to be involved in civil war.
2. The ceremony and formality of the language in *Richard II* creates a distance between what the characters are saying and what they are actually thinking and feeling. As poetry is more formal than prose, the characters engage in public rather than private speech. (See Michael Mullin's essay.)
3. An Elizabethan audience would have been aware of Richard's guilt from the very beginning and would have discerned the discrepancy between his words and feelings in I, i. The modern director, however, must make certain that his less-informed audience is aware of a tension between the characters in I, i, even if the text of the speeches does not directly inform them of the events causing that tension.

56   The Tragedy of King Richard the Second

Twelfth Night or What You Will

The First Part of King Henry the Fourth

The Tragedy of King Richard the Second

The Tragedy of King Richard the Second 57

The First Part of King Henry the Fourth

The Second Part of King Henry the Fourth

The Life of King Henry the Fifth

4. This scene serves as an extended allegory for the situation then current in England and, indeed, as a commentary on the action of the entire play. The Gardener and his men liken England to an untended garden being ruined by the neglect of its royal caretaker. The Gardener is also used to inform the audience—and the eavesdropping Queen—of Richard's defeat and fall. Often likened to the role of a chorus, the Gardener and his men comment impartially on Richard's failure to prune his kingdom of troublesome weeds and on Bolingbroke's success. In spite of the Queen's stern rebuke, the Gardener's continued compassion for her signals that the audience, too, should view the dethronement of the King with sympathy.

5. In the first two acts, the audience sees Richard as a young, extravagant, indecisive, and unjust king. It becomes apparent he has, in fact, ordered the murder of his uncle, the Duke of Gloucester, and that he permits a loyal follower, Mowbray, to take the blame and suffer banishment. Richard vindictively confiscates the estates of his chief accuser, his cousin Bolingbroke. In short, Richard gives his audience ample justification for disliking him and for his eventual dethronement. But in the last three acts, Shakespeare reveals Richard's inner personality in extraordinarily rich poetry. We discover he is aware of his weaknesses and selfishness, and that he had a conscience, all of which heighten his tragedy.

THE FIRST PART OF KING HENRY THE FOURTH

INTRODUCTION TO THE PLAY

Its title and the fact that it is categorized as one of Shakespeare's "history" plays should not mislead us. *The First Part of King Henry the Fourth* is not so much about the character for whom it is named as it is about Henry's son of the same name, or Prince Hal as he is more familiarly called. But the play also is about Henry Percy, nicknamed Hotspur, who was the charismatic leader of the Yorkist rebels and with whom Prince Hal was compared, not always favorably. And it is about the irrepressible Sir John Falstaff, the sottish reprobate whom Shakespeare developed into perhaps the greatest comic character in all English literature. Thus, the political events leading up to the ostensible climax of the play—the battle of Shrewsbury—must share the spotlight with the richly varied troupe of characters Shakespeare introduces to his audience in this play, and with the personal dramas he delineates for a number of them.

Historically and dramatically, *1 Henry IV* follows hard on the heels of *Richard II*. The events mentioned in the play take place during the thirteen-month period between the battles of Holmedon (June 1402) and Shrewsbury (July 1403), meaning that Henry has reigned—at best shakily—for just a little over a year. Dramatically, the link between the two plays is even more immediate, for the opening lines of *1 Henry IV* discuss the very promise Henry makes in the last lines of *Richard II* to make a pilgrimage to the Holy Land to expiate his guilt for having usurped the English throne and indirectly provided the murder of his predecessor. We learn immediately that the anticipated crusade has had to be postponed because there is rebellion among the supporters of the former king and even insubordination among the nobles who had earlier allied themselves with King Henry, then called Bolingbroke and still referred to as such by his enemies.

In addition to King Henry/Bolingbroke, only three other characters are "carried over" from *Richard II*, and all three are members of the Yorkist faction: the Earl of Northumberland, his son Hotspur, and Sir Stephen Scroop, now Archbishop of York. Compare this small number with the fully one dozen characters from this play who are carried over into *2 Henry IV*, including Prince Hal, his brother Prince John of Lancaster, Scroop, Lady Percy, and such notable comic characters as Falstaff, Bardolph, Poins, and Mistress Quickly.

American students often have difficulty keeping track of the characters in Shakespeare's history plays, especially since the characters usually are referred to by a shortened version of their titles; for example, the Earl of Northumberland = Northumberland, the Earl of Worcester = Worcester. It is sometimes helpful not only to become familiar with this method of identification, but to group the characters according to political or other affiliations: Westmoreland and Blunt are loyal to the King; Edmund Mortimer, Owen Glendower, the Earl of Douglas, and the Archbishop of York are allied to the rebel faction led by the Percy family (Northumberland, Worcester, and Hotspur). Similarly, the underworld characters associated with Falstaff may be grouped together: Poins, Gadshill, Peto, Bardolph. Marking the list of actors at the head of the play accordimg to these groupings should provide an easy reference as you read through it, or underlining the speech headings by different colored markers may help code the characters. Of course, few of these difficulties occur in watching a performance, where the personalities of the actors as well as the costumes the actors wear greatly aid the audience in making proper identifications.

Notice how Shakespeare's characterization of individuals appears to vary from play to play as does their relative importance to the events of that play. For example, in *Richard II*, the Earl of Northumberland is Bolingbroke's staunchest and most ruthless ally, but in this play, as Henry's enemy, he is so irresolute that he fails to raise an army in support of his brother and son at the crucial battle of Shrewsbury. In *Richard II*, Hotspur has but two cameo appearances (only one in the television version) and speaks only six or seven brief lines. In this play he is the martial and marital hero, despite his disloyalty, and is eclipsed only at the very end when Prince Hal sheds his prodigal image, matures into a dependable heir apparent, and kills Hotspur at Shrewsbury. Prince Hal himself never even appears in *Richard II* and is referred to only once by his despairing father as an "unthrifty son" who frequents London taverns "with unrestrained loose companions" and robs passers-by (V, iii, 1-19). In this play, it is Hal's emergence as a worthy prince that is a major dramatic emphasis.

You should resist the temptation to dismiss as mere interludes of comic relief the boisterous carousing and boozy briganding of Prince Hal, Falstaff, and their ne'er-do-well companions, Poins, Bardolph, Peto, and Gadshill. These scenes are an essential feature of the play, not only for the breadth of characterization they allow Shakespeare to display but also as the medium in which Hal's almost miraculous transformation takes place. In the beginning, Prince Hal is depicted as an intemperate swain whose ventures have alienated him from his father. Moreover, while Shakespeare accords Hal more attention than he does his father, Hal is neither the colorful rascal that is Falstaff nor the model of a dutiful son and military hero that is Hotspur. Hal suffers by comparison to both. And it is from these inauspicious beginnings that we watch Hal's emergence as a true and noble prince—the future King Henry V.

In his essay, "The Trials of King and Prince," Jay Halio carefully leads the reader through each major phase and turning point of the play, highlighting the interrelationships of diverse persons and themes at each stage in the proceedings and bringing the whole to its conclusion at Shrewsbury. We are brought to a clear understanding why this battle is not only the climax to the historical and political struggles described in the play, but also to the personal dramas each major character undergoes. Having read Halio's comments, you should, as you read the play and view the televised production of it, be able to retrace the ingenious development of plot and character for which Shakespeare is justly famous.

LESSON ASSIGNMENTS

In order to get the most out of the specially designed introductory material and to appreciate the unique qualities of the play itself, Jay Halio strongly recommends that you prepare yourself in the following manner:
- Read the synopsis of *1 Henry IV* in this guide.
- Read the text of *1 Henry IV*.
- Read "*The Trials of King and Prince: The First Part of King Henry the Fourth*" by Jay Halio in this guide.
- View the television production.
- Complete the Self-test at the end of this lesson.

LEARNING OBJECTIVES

After completing the reading assignments and viewing the televised drama production, you should be able to:
1. Compare Henry IV's private problems with his public concerns for the welfare of England.
2. Define the major aspects of Falstaff's wit and wisdom and describe their attraction/repulsion for Prince Hal amd for you.
3. Describe Prince Hal's dilemma in fulfilling his obligation and paying the debt as the Prince of Wales and in following his natural impulses. Describe the way he resolves this dilemma.
4. Identify the major characters (Hotspur, Henry IV, Hal, Falstaff, Glendower, Worcester, and others) and place them on a scale ranging from extreme romanticism to extreme pragmatism. Discuss why it is difficult to place some characters at a single point on this scale.
5. Define the relationship between scenes in the Boar's Head Tavern and scenes in the court and elsewhere that deal with major historical events.
6. Define the elements of Hotspur's tragedy in contrast to Hal's triumph.

SYNOPSIS OF THE PLAY
ACT I

KING HENRY IV postpones his crusade to Jerusalem when he learns that rebellion is raging in his kingdom. GLENDOWER, the Welsh rebel, has defeated the army of LORD MORTIMER (Earl of March), but the heroism of young HARRY PERCY (HOTSPUR) has ended a Scottish uprising. King Henry wishes that Hotspur were his son; his own son, PRINCE HAL, is leading a life of "riot and dishonor."

In a disreputable tavern, we meet Prince Hal and his fat, amoral friend, SIR JOHN FALSTAFF. Another friend, POINS, proposes a robbery. Hal is reluctant, but Poins takes him aside and reveals his plan: to rob Falstaff and his cronies after Falstaff robs the pilgrims. Poins leaves and Hal discloses his true feelings: Soon he will surprise the world by renouncing this disreputable behavior and assuming his royal responsibilities.

King Henry holds a council of war, demanding that Hotspur deliver his prisoners to court. Hotspur, in turn, demands that the King ransom Lord Mortimer from the Welsh. Henry vehemently refuses. Left alone, Hotspur, his father (the Earl of NORTHUMBERLAND), and his uncle (WORCESTOR), plan a rebellion. They are incensed that the King has not given them better treatment since they helped him overthrow King Richard II.

ACT II

The morning of the robbery dawns. Waiting for the pilgrims, Falstaff finds that Poins has hidden his horse, and then that Poins and the Prince are not at hand. Falstaff and two friends ambush the caravan anyway and are promptly robbed of their gains by Hal and Poins, in disguise.

At home, Hotspur reads a letter from a lord who declines to join the rebellion. He is interrupted by his wife, KATE, who scolds him for neglecting her. Preparing to ride off, he promises to send for her.

Egged on by Hal and Poins, Falstaff invents a wild battle with a band of bloodthirsty cutthroats who took the gold from him. When they reveal the truth, he claims that he knew it was the Prince all along. News arrives from court, and Hal and Falstaff stage an impromptu play in which they assume and then exchange the roles of King and Prince confronting each other over the Prince's disreputable friends. The game is interrupted by the arrival of the sheriff, looking for Falstaff, but Prince Hal shields him.

ACT III

In Glendower's palace in Wales, the Welsh chief meets with Hotspur, Worcester, and Mortimer (who, having married Glendower's daughter, has now joined the Percys' rebellion) to discuss how to divide England after their victory. Hotspur rashly makes fun of Glendower's claims of magical powers. Finally, the men pass a brief interval of peace with their wives.

King Henry and Prince Hal confront each other, and the King accuses Hal of being so degenerate as to endanger their family's grasp on the throne. They reconcile and Hal is given a command in the army.

More trouble in the tavern: Falstaff accuses Mistress Quickly of having picked his pockets. Hal reveals that he himself is the culprit and shames Falstaff for having monstrously exaggerated the worth of what was stolen. Falstaff then learns even worse news: Hal has gotten him a command of foot in the army.

ACT IV

At the rebel camp near Shrewsbury the leaders of the insurrection argue about when to attack, with Hotspur insisting on immediate action. When King Henry's emissary requests a list of grievances, Hotspur emotionally charges King Henry with ingratitude toward those who helped him seize the throne. Calming himself, he promises to send Worcester to discuss terms with the King the next day.

The ARCHBISHOP OF YORK worries about the possibility that some rebels may not appear for battle. Sure enough, word comes that neither Northumberland nor Glendower can fight at Shrewsbury.

Falstaff, now leading a starving army of tattered soldiers, is three hundred pounds richer from bribes offered by those able to buy their way out of his service. The Prince deplores the appearance of Falstaff's army but urges him to hurry to the battle anyway.

ACT V

Worcester takes his grievances to the King. Hal proposes trial by single combat with Hotspur and the King offers a promise of peace if the rebels will yield. Worcester, however, conceals the offers from Hotspur.

The Battle of Shrewsbury rages. In one encounter, Prince Hal saves his father from the Scottish leader, Douglas. The battle climaxes in a brutal fight between Hal and Hotspur, in which Hal kills his rival. When Hal departs, Falstaff, who has been feigning death nearby, gets up and stabs the dead Hotspur, then picks up the corpse to claim credit. Hal, glad to see fat Sir John alive, permits the lie. The day ends in complete victory for the King.

The Trials of King and Prince:
The First Part of King Henry the Fourth

Jay L. Halio

The deposition and death of Richard II, in Shakespeare's vision of history, put England under a curse from which she did not expiate herself for nearly a century. The immediate consequences of the events that led to Richard's downfall are dramatized in the closing scenes of *Richard II*, the first of four plays that make up the tetralogy sometimes called the "Henriad." Rebellion is rife. Conspiracy to unseat Henry IV takes shape, for example, when the Duke of York's son and others plot to kill the king. Fortunately for Henry, through York's intervention—he is willing to let the full rigor of the law fall upon his own son—this conspiracy is foiled; but others break out. Those loyal to the new king bring word of victories over rebellious nobles such as Salisbury and Oxford, but the insurrection in Gloucester still rages, and the town of Cirencester is in flames. These events all herald the unquiet times of the reign of Henry IV.

The First Part of King Henry the Fourth opens with Henry visibly shaken and nearly worn out from fighting battles to keep the throne he has taken from Richard. Shakespeare shows him much aged by "the furious close of civil butchery" (I, i, 13). For the moment, he believes he has restored sufficient order so that he can fulfill a year-old pledge to lead a crusade to atone for his sins against Richard. But this hope is soon dashed. Westmoreland reports on a fresh defeat in Wales: Edmund Mortimer, Earl of March, leading his troops "against the irregular and wild Glendower," has been badly defeated and himself taken prisoner (I, i, 34-42). Even the good news of the victory at Holmedon over the Scots carries a sting. The valiant Harry Percy, "Hotspur," who has won the battle over the Earl of Douglas, refuses to give the king most of the noblemen he has taken prisoner. Henry interprets this act as insubordination—or worse—and at once plans to deal with it. It appears that Hotspur's uncle, the Earl of Worcester, has fired the young man up to this behavior. As we shall see, Worcester is Henry's chief antagonist in the events that follow, most like him in political sense and outlook. Breaking off his "holy purpose to Jerusalem," Henry decides to hold a council meeting at Windsor Castle within a few days to consider these problems (I, i, 100-108).

Act I, scene iii shows the results of Henry's decision. Assembled before him at court are the northern nobles—Northumberland, Worcester, and Hotspur—along with others, such as Sir Walter Blunt, who carried the news of Holmedon and supports Hotspur's account of what happened. To Henry's opening stance, designed to assert his full majesty and authority, Worcester first opposes himself, reminding Henry of the Percys' help in placing him on the throne. He does not get very far: Henry, sensing "danger and disobedience" in his eyes, summarily dismisses him, preferring to deal directly with Hotspur and his father, whom he feels perhaps he can manage better without Worcester.

Hotspur denies that he ever refused his prisoners to the king. He became impatient with the popinjay who came to claim them and threw him out. But Henry is not taken in by this excuse: "Why, yet he doth deny his prisoners," he counters, and remarks upon the conditions that Hotspur has set down for their surrender (I, iii, 77ff). This argument brings matters to a head, for the major condition that Hotspur requires is the ransom of his brother-in-law, Edmund Mortimer, from the Welshman Glendower. Henry refuses. His reasons are that Mortimer is a traitor, has betrayed the lives of those he led against Glendower, and has topped his treason off by marrying Glendower's daughter! But Henry may have a more significant reason to let Mortimer starve "upon the barren mountains." After the King departs with his ultimatum—"Send us your prisoners, or you will hear of it" (I, iii, 124)—Northumberland and Worcester reveal that Richard II, who was childless, actually had named Mortimer heir to his throne (I, iii, 145-52). Henry thus has in Mortimer a counterclaimant to the crown he wears and is trying hard to keep. Although Shakespeare confuses or combines Edmund Mortimer, the Fifth Earl of March (1391-1424), named by Richard as heir, with his uncle, Sir Edmund Mortimer (1376-1409), who married Glendower's daughter, the dramatic point is the same: Henry has the best reason in the world to discredit Mortimer and keep him out of the picture, for the last thing he needs during this period of turmoil is a pretender to the throne.

What happens in the rest of this scene is important not only for setting in motion the major political and historical forces that occupy a large part of the plot, but also for establishing the characters of the young, fiery Hotspur and the other Percys. Here again Shakespeare alters history to make Hotspur younger than Henry IV and a foil to Henry's son, Prince Hal. Hotspur, his quick temper flashing out at the King's harsh words, swears that far from remaining silent about Mortimer, as the King demanded, he'll holler "Mortimer" in the king's ear when he lies asleep, or train a starling to speak nothing but "Mortimer" and give it to the King (I, iii, 220-5). His father and uncle have a difficult time getting Hotspur to calm down so that they can devise their plans. Notice that during this dialogue, Shakespeare very carefully separates Hotspur from the other two in recapitulating the part the Percy family had in dethroning Richard and helping Henry to his place. Although Hotspur was present at Berkeley Castle and pledged support to Henry Bolingbroke when he arrived there to claim his rights from Richard, the young man is otherwise made to seem entirely innocent of the plot that eventually succeeded in crowning Henry king. If Hotspur is to be "the theme of honor's tongue," as Henry earlier described him (I, i, 81), he must not be guilty of those crimes from which, as Hotspur says, the time yet serves wherein his father and his uncle may redeem their banished honors and restore their reputations (I, iii, 180-82). Thus we are given Hotspur's optimistic view of the action that will take place.

Worcester, the chief schemer, does not so embroider his plots, although he recognizes Hotspur's usefulness as their champion. His political insight penetrates to the heart of the Percys' relationship with the King, who, in Worcester's judgment, "will always think him in our debt," and therefore always suspect their discontent until he has found a "time to pay us home" (I, iii, 283-85). Consequently, Worcester has been busy developing some initiatives. He tells Hotspur to free his prisoners without ransom and use Douglas's son as a further means to gain Scotland's support. At the same time, Northumberland will enlist the already disaffected Archbishop of York and so mount a strong head, together with Mortimer, Glendower, and the Scots, against the forces of the King. Thus the Percy rebellion is hatched, to the evident delight of its youngest member, who can't wait to get into battle again.

Cutting across the panorama of history that has begun to unfold, or rather slicing into it, are the scenes with Prince Hal, Falstaff, and their cronies. While they provide much of the rich comedy in the play, these scenes serve other significant purposes, such as providing a different perspective on the values that the important historical personages are prepared to fight and die for. But it is necessary not to miss the fun—something many people at first may find difficult if they view Falstaff mainly as a dirty old man who misleads the Prince of Wales and engages in unsavory escapades that discredit them both. Part of Falstaff's humor lies in his consummate mimicry: He beautifully parodies, for example, the penitent sinner (I, ii, 76-92) and the stylish, euphuistic courtier (II, iv, 380 ff). Much comedy lies also in the conduct of his escapades and the way he deals with their consequences. But the best part of his fun is his quick and ready wit, capable of turning an attack upon himself into an attack upon his accuser: His imagination is so fertile and his language so equal to his imagination that he has remained a delight to theatergoers and students for centuries. It is not often enough emphasized that some of the best English prose ever written is the prose that Falstaff and Hal speak, especially in the early scenes of *1 Henry IV*.

Their very first lines typify the exuberance and quickness of their dialogue. Falstaff awakens from an afternoon nap on a bench in the Prince's apartment (as the scene usually is staged) and simply inquires about the hour. The answer he gets is without doubt far in excess of what the question requires, but it immediately establishes the nature of the relationship between Hal and his friend. "What a devil hast thou to do with the time of day?" (I, ii, 5-6),

Hal demands. Falstaff agrees: He is by no means a "day" person. On the contrary, he only truly comes alive after the sun has set, the moon is out, and nocturnal adventures are afoot. But (again typically) before he finishes his response, he puts the Prince on the defensive instead of himself; for the Prince is out of grace and will have none. Moreover, Falstaff indicates from the outset that he is fully aware of the Prince's responsibilities as heir apparent to the crown and of the day when he must become king. The first of their scenes together clearly foreshadows the end of a relationship that occurs in *2 Henry IV*, but one that Falstaff will do everything to prolong—even into Hal's reign as King Henry V—if he can.

What, we may ask, is Falstaff's hold upon the young prince? Is it the enjoyment of good times, the exchange of repartee, the easy-going life of the London underworld? Or is there something more—a rebellion on Hal's part, too, against his father, the King, a rebellion such as many sons of the powerful or wealthy experience as they grow up and face having to assume a position they resent—or even fear? That King Henry is worried and upset about his son's way of life we know from as early as *Richard II*, where Henry asks, "Can no man tell me of my unthrifty son?" (V, iii, l); he has not seen him in three months. Henry also recognizes his son's behavior as a kind of retribution against him: "If any plague hang over us, 'tis he." In the first scene of *1 Henry IV* the King again ruefully acknowledges his son's dissolute behavior and bad reputation, when he bitterly compares him with Northumberland's son, also named Henry, and wishes that some fairy had exchanged the children in their cradles so that the King could claim a nobler scion for his own (I, i, 78-90). Shakespeare thus presents both public and private sources of concern for Henry IV; the relationships between these two realms of action culminate in the Battle of Shrewsbury that concludes the play but not Henry's reign, which goes on for another dozen troubled years.

The plot to rob the pilgrims at Gad's Hill parallels and contrasts with the Percys' plot against King Henry, and it is deliberately placed in the sequence of events between the first and third scenes of Act I. In this way, Shakespeare suggests that the fabric of Henry's rule is being rent at every level of English life. Anarchy threatens on all sides, it seems. When invited to participate in the escapade at Gad's Hill, Hal at first demurs: The "true prince" will not, as Falstaff wants, "(for recreation sake) prove a false thief" (I, ii, 145). But after Falstaff leaves, Ned Poins, who has broached the plot to them, persuades Hal to join in by suggesting a plot within the plot: Hal and he will don disguises and contrive matters so that they will not be present when the pilgrims are robbed. Instead they will set upon Falstaff and the others afterward and steal the booty from them. This, Poins promises, will be an excellent subject for a jest when they all gather later at the Boar's Head Tavern and listen to Falstaff's immense lies about what happened. Checking carefully with Poins on the details of the plan, Hal agrees to join in after all.

It may be worth noting that here, as later in *2 Henry IV*, it is Poins, not Falstaff, who misleads the Prince, at least in the escapades that Shakespeare dramatizes. But regardless of who is the principal "corrupter" of the heir apparent, the question again imposes itself: Why does Hal do these things? He gives us his own explanation in a soliloquy at the end of the second scene of Act I. He knows them all, he says, and for the time is willing to go along with his companions' unbridled foolishness. He is willing to do so, that is, so that when the time comes for him to assert his true self, he will utterly astonish those who have accepted his reputation for recklessness. His "reformation" then will win him more credit and more wonder in men's eyes than had he never consorted with the underworld. The metaphors Hal uses here vividly convey his meaning: He will "imitate the sun" and for a while allow "the base contagious clouds" to obscure "his beauty from the world" until he is pleased "again to be himself." Or, "like bright metal on a sullen ground," his reformation will outshine his fault the better for having a foil to set it off. Hal's words suggest that he is indeed his father's son; he has a calculating, political bent that has put off some critics, because it apparently contradicts the more engaging, humane aspects of his character. But this interpretation misses the complexity of Hal's character and the way that Shakespeare begins to prepare him—and us, the audience—for the role that the Prince will later assume as king. The debt he owes is one he never incurred, just as the world he lives in is not of his making. But he already has the maturity to recognize that, like it or not, he does have an obligation, and he will fulfill it. While he can, however, he will enjoy the holidays that his present condition affords him, recognizing at the same time that if all life were playing holiday, as Falstaff seems to do, then for Hal "to sport would be as tedious as to work."

This holiday spirit and its representation occupy almost the whole of Act II and reach a climax in the great Boar's Head Tavern scene. As the Percy clan gathers its forces for the rebellion against the King, the robbers gather together at Gad's Hill for the assault upon the pilgrims going to Canterbury. The punning dialogue in II, i suggests the levity that will characterize the episode and continues the play upon "true-false" (II, i, 89ff) that has become a leitmotiv. The fun with Falstaff begins as Poins hides the knight's horse and forces him, huffing and puffing, to climb the hill on foot. As the robbers ready themselves for the attack, Poins and Hal move away from the rest with the excuse that they will establish a back-up position if the travelers get away. The pilgrims soon enter. Falstaff leads the charge, waving his sword and shouting in a manner that utterly frightens the victims but delights the audience with its ironies: "Ah, whoreson caterpillars! bacon-fed knaves! they hate us youth" (II, ii, 78-79). If Falstaff by these bizarre cries means somehow to throw suspicion off himself, in another sense part of what he yells is true, for he is clearly the "youngest" of all in outlook and behavior, and "young men must live" (II, ii, 83). Immediately afterward, as Falstaff and the others are dividing the loot, Poins and Hal pounce upon them, scare them off, and themselves carry away the booty.

But the best fun lies ahead at the Boar's Head, where they meet again according to plan. Hal is in his cups, having drunk deep with "a leash of drawers" (II, iv, 6ff); but though he is their "sworn brother" and can call them all by their first names, he is still the Prince of Wales, however hearty the fellowship. His joking with poor Francis may strike us as cruel—an indirect manifestation, perhaps, of the pressures Hal is experiencing (the debt he never promised) or of the guilt he feels for his present comportment. But Shakespeare's audience, for all its poetic sensibility, would have roared with laughter at the helpless and hopelessly conflicted waiter, who finally stands paralyzed with confusion, until Hal sends him on his way. Falstaff meanwhile has arrived, but before he enters, Hal comments on the fun with Francis and then remarks: "I am not yet of Percy's mind, the Hotspur of the North; he that kills me some six or seven dozen of Scots at breakfast, washes his hands, and says to his wife, 'Fie upon this quiet life! I want work' " (II, iv, 97-100). The interjection shows that Hal is aware of how others may be contrasting the two young men; at the same time, it reflects the short scene just before this one between Hotspur and his wife. Hal is not *yet* of Percy's mind; later he may have to be.

Falstaff stomps in, calling for sack (his favorite drink), and swearing against all cowards. He is at his best here: thrusting and parrying with his wit to excellent advantage, as in his exchange with Poins, whom he calls a coward (II, iv, 134ff). Typically, he takes the offensive rather than risk having to defend himself for not showing up with the spoils from the robbery. Not sure exactly what happened, he may have some suspicions about Hal and Poins, and these could explain his extraordinary behavior in recounting the events at Gad's Hill. If his fantastic lies (which exhibit one aspect of his fertile imagination) are calculated to exasperate the Prince and thereby extract from him a true account of what happened, they certainly succeed. "Gross as a mountain, open, palpable," as Hal calls these fabrications, can they really hope to fool anyone? When Hal exposes the truth and challenges his friend to find some "device" to hide him from shame, Falstaff responds: he knew them all the time! It was not for him to kill the heir apparent. "Beware instinct," Falstaff says, "The lion will not touch the true prince" (II, iv, 257). He then claims to have been a coward "upon instinct." Whatever we may think of his behavior—and some excellent arguments have been made to show that charges against Falstaff for cowardice are entirely irrelevant, since he never accepts the premises upon which valor or cowardice are decided—we must recognize the finesse with which Falstaff handles himself here. The main thing is that the gang has the money, and the revelry may begin in earnest. A *play extempore* will be just the ticket.

But before they can get started, or even decide on a subject, they are interrupted, and Falstaff is sent to deal with the messenger from King Henry's court. Thus even the saturnalian world of the Boar's Head Tavern is not so thoroughly insulated from the iron world of history that it cannot suffer intrusions—reminders to us as to Prince Hal that there is another sphere of activity to which we owe dues. When Falstaff reenters, he brings news of impending civil war. Hal must go to the court in the morning and speak with his father. In preparation for that event, Hal agrees to rehearse an answer to his father's anticipated reprimands. To Hostess Quickly's delight—and ours—Falstaff plays Henry IV and brings Hal to a reckoning. Parodying the euphuistic style once fashionable at court, Falstaff lightly scolds the wayward prince and in the process begins an *apologia pro vita sua* (an apology for, or defense of, his own way of life) (II, iv, 401-9). Suddenly Hal decides to reverse their positions and changes Falstaff's highly flattering description of himself to terms that are anything but complimentary (II, iv, 425ff). Falstaff (as Hal) feigns puzzlement, then confesses he knows the man, but rejects the adverse criticisms. So his *apologia* continues, here more earnestly and more movingly. The threat of banishment, always implicit, comes out in the open. Falstaff's appeal is to banish all the others, but not "sweet," "kind," "true," "valiant," "old" Jack Falstaff. "Banish plump Jack," he concludes, "and banish all the world!" (II, iv, 456).

The challenge now is to the Prince, and he accepts it: "I do, I will." But whether Falstaff hears him is not clear; certainly he does not take it in, though we must. Much, however, will occur before the banishment is actually carried out at the end of *2 Henry IV*. Meanwhile, distracting the characters on stage and creating much confusion and consternation, the sheriff and the watch knock on the door, aroused by the hue and cry after Falstaff and the robbers. Confident in Hal's protection, or at least putting on a brave front, Falstaff is allowed to hide while Hal deals with the officers. Once again, the world of reality breaks into the world of Falstaffian revel, that urban pastoral to which the Prince retreats as a temporary refuge from the cares he inevitably must shoulder. His moment of severest trial approaches, as events leading to armed confrontation between the Percys and the King gather momentum. Perforce Hal will be in the vanguard of the battle, once he has faced his father and declared his true feelings.

Before that important event, we witness the marshaling of the rebel factions in Wales. New aspects of Hotspur's character, some of them first seen in the brief episode with his wife in II, iii, are revealed along with the introduction of the magician Glendower, his son-in-law Mortimer, and his daughter. In a play that deals with a wide variety of romantics, few of them simply rendered, Glendower is unquestionably the most extreme. Claiming that great signs and wonders attended his nativity, Glendower quickly antagonizes Hotspur, whose otherwise romantic nature refuses to accept such prodigies as having anything to do with the Welshman's birth or subsequent accomplishments. His hardheaded attitude repeatedly manifests itself, especially in the quarrel over the division of the realm (a realm that is hardly theirs to divide, in any case). When Glendower finally relents, Hotspur shows his true magnanimity. Though in the way of the bargain he may "cavil on the ninth part of a hair" (III, i, 138), in friendship his generosity is boundless. Hotspur's lack of tact, nevertheless, earns him lectures from both Mortimer and Worcester, and it becomes evident that all is not well in the rebel camp. The down-to-earth side of Hotspur's nature is again revealed in the dialogue with the ladies. Although neither can speak the other's language, Mortimer and his wife have convinced themselves that they are head over heels in love with each other. In contrast to the "romance" of their relationship, Hotspur and his wife engage in the realistic byplay of a couple whose long and deep affection for each other finds expression in witty teasing, sexual and otherwise. Their devotion also underlines the tragic aspects of Hotspur's experience as it unfolds throughout the drama.

Just as Hotspur's uncle lectures him in III, i, Hal's father lectures the Prince in the following scene, although there are important differences. Hal more readily accepts some, though by no means all, of the accusations against him, and he appears sincerely moved by his father's deep concern. Hal's misdeeds appear to Henry to be a heavenly retribution against him (as well they might be). Though Hal reassures his father that things really are not as bad as they seem, Henry goes on to warn his son that he is following Richard II's disastrous example. By contrast, Henry offers his own behavior (not quite borne out by reference back to *Richard II*), which was carefully calculated to win people's hearts, not their disgust or disaffection. Between the Prince and his father, as we know from Hal's soliloquy in I, ii, no difference really exists in either political means or ends: both intend to use others' performances as well as their own to best advantage. Hence, Hal promises not only to be more himself (III, ii, 92), but to benefit from Hotspur's reputation when the time comes for them to meet in battle.

Despite their rhetoric (they necessarily use the "high" style, or idiom, appropriate to their station and to the dramatic situation), father and son, King and Prince, are both pragmatists in the world where chivalry is, if not quite dead, then surely on its last legs. If those legs are Hotspur's, as they clearly are, then it has the most brilliant exponent imaginable. But chivalry is nonetheless doomed, and Prince Hal, as we shall see, fittingly pronounces its epitaph. Understood another way, if Hotspur is more than eager "To pluck bright honor from the pale-faced moon, / Or dive into the bottom of the deep, / . . . And pluck up drowned honor by the locks" (I, iii, 202-5), Hal indulges in no such flamboyance, biding his time till the right moment. Hotspur is but his "factor" (III, ii, 147), his agent or deputy, to corner the market on noble deeds so that when Hal is ready to redeem himself in his father's and the world's eyes, all he must do is vanquish Percy and claim his honor for his own. Cheered by his son's convincing determination and vow of loyalty, Henry prepares to meet his foes very soon at Shrewsbury.

Though Hotspur and Falstaff may share some romantic qualities, such as a childlike and single-minded devotion to what they thoroughly believe in, those very beliefs stand diametrically opposed to each other. In his advocacy of honor at any cost, Hotspur demonstrates his romantic commitment to a creed outworn. In his refusal to grow up and behave in a manner more consistent with his white hairs, Falstaff shows a similar childlike attribute. Both attributes may eventually prove fatal. In the preparations for war, and in the conduct of that war, however, the sharpest contrasts emerge, and between Hotspur and Falstaff stands the Prince. But as the dialectic of this play unfolds, we see that Hal is always his own man, not an amalgam or composite of their two radically incompatible value systems. These two characters finally do not so much define Hal as set off his true qualities, exactly as they are intended to do, if we may extrapolate from Hal's first soliloquy.

The Prince's meeting with his father in III, ii is a pivotal point in the action. While the three strands of the plot have hitherto proceeded along mainly separate lines, they now begin to converge and will reach a climax at Shrewsbury. Preparations for battle begin apace. Hal arrives at the Boar's Head Tavern, where Falstaff is consorting with Bardolph, Mistress Quickly, and others, mulling over his fallen-away state and complaining about his pocket having been picked. His language, as richly textured as ever, and as full of wit, triumphs over Bardolph's carbuncled face, Mrs. Quickly's outraged simplicity, and Hal's attempts to catch him out. But even Jack Falstaff must abandon this merry tavern life and prepare for war. Once again, the Prince has been "good angel" to his friend: the Gad's Hill money has been paid back, and Hal has procured Falstaff "a charge of foot" (III, iii, 69-78). Naturally wishing it had been a charge of horse, Falstaff's immediate thought is to find "one that can steal well . . . a fine thief of the age of two-and-twenty or thereabouts!" (III, iii, 180-81). For Falstaff, the war is more than anything else an opportunity for personal profit.

Shakespeare dramatizes this attitude and contrasts it with others in the next two acts. For example, Falstaff ponders how he has used, or abused, the king's press, or his authority to conscript soldiers for the king's army (IV, ii, 11ff). Seizing first upon the wealthy and physically able, he has allowed these "toasts-and-butter" to buy themselves out of service and has pocketed over three hundred pounds in the process. In their place, he has rounded up the poor, the halt, and the lame, most of them from prisons. They are such a wretched lot that Westmoreland and Hal openly wonder at their condition. Falstaff's response indicates another aspect of his attitude: "Tut, tut! good enough to toss; food for powder, food for powder. They'll fill a pit as well as better" (IV, ii, 62-64). If men are being led into battle where death is certain, does it really matter, Falstaff suggests, what their condition is? May it not even be better to sacrifice society's rabble rather than the cream of its young manhood? Falstaff's cynicism, coupled with his self-aggrandizement, may put us off; but given the insights of one who sees beneath chivalry's golden coats to the harsh realities of bloody battles, his point of view has its own clear rationale.

As in most things, Falstaff's rationale for fighting battles is at the opposite pole from Hotspur's. In the rebel camp, the news is not good. Northumberland (Hotspur's father) is ill and cannot bring his troops. Glendower and Mortimer also fail to make the rendezvous, suggesting that the cracks in the rebel cause, glimpsed earlier, have split wider. Worcester is visibly concerned by these apparent defections, but Hotspur sees advantages. It may be imprudent to risk all their forces in a single battle; moreover, others will think them confident in their cause—contrary to Worcester's fears—if they venture forth with a smaller army. And the glory in the victory will be so much the greater, the fewer there are to share it.

Hotspur still seems the "king of honor," as Douglas calls him (IV, i, 10), but the rivalry between him and the Prince of Wales here breaks out in earnest. Sir Richard Vernon glowingly describes Hal and his troops preparing for battle: "Glittering in golden coats like images; / As full of spirit as the month of May / And gorgeous as the sun at midsummer" (IV, i, 100-2). When Vernon comes to the description of Hal rising from the ground "like feathered Mercury" to vault with ease into his saddle, Hotspur cannot stand it any longer and cuts him off. Anxious to get started, he and Douglas later argue with Worcester and Vernon about launching the battle that very evening, before the King has fully prepared to fight. As the quarrel continues, Sir Walter Blunt enters "with gracious offers from the king" (IV, iii, 30), but Hotspur takes this opportunity to rehearse the many grievances he has against Henry (IV, iii, 52-105). Unwilling, nevertheless, to break off the possibility of reconciliation, Hotspur agrees to parley with the King by sending his uncle, Worcester, to him the next morning.

The meeting is not a successful one, owing mainly to Worcester's bitterness, suspicion, and final treachery. He proclaims at length the injuries the Percys have suffered at Henry's hands and antagonizes the King. Hal intervenes. Reminding everyone of the price the battle will cost in human lives, and praising Hotspur for his chivalrous deeds and well-earned reputation, the Prince offers to take the odds against young Percy and meet him in a single combat, thereby to decide the conflict. But Henry will not allow it. Instead, he proposes terms of peace so generous that even Worcester, on his way back to Hotspur with Vernon, has to recognize "the liberal and kind offer of the king" (V, ii, 2). It is an offer that Hotspur never gets to hear. While the King may excuse youthful excess, Worcester fears he can never forgive older heads like theirs and persuades Vernon not to reveal the proposed amnesty. Accepting what he takes to be the King's defiance, and hearing Vernon's fresh praises of the Prince, Hotspur impatiently assembles his troops, confident in victory and certainly in glory, as he shouts "Esperancé! Percy! and set on" (V, ii, 96).

Unlike Hotspur's lofty sentiments or Hal's quiet confidence and humility, Falstaff's concern remains primarily for his own skin. If it is a time for honor and high chivalry, he is not impressed. His soliloquy upon honor probes various implications of the term and concludes, since it is of no sensible or material good whatever, that honor is merely air, an empty name or "scutcheon"—and he will have "none of it" (V, i, 129-39). During the battle Douglas kills Sir Walter Blunt, and Falstaff mutters over the corpse, "There's honor for you!" (V, iii, 32). On his part, he has led his ragamuffins to the slaughter, not three of one hundred fifty left alive, "and they are for the town's end, to beg during life" (V, iii, 37-38). Later, he counterfeits death rather than fight with Douglas and justifies his behavior by proclaiming "the better part of valor is discretion" (V, iv, 118).

By disguising many others in his colors, Henry appears to practice a similar "discretion," much to the confusion and disgust of Douglas, who more than once believes he has won the battle by killing the King. Henry's crafty device is more political than craven, for when Douglas finally does catch up with him, he does not shirk the encounter. Finding the true king recalls the "true prince" dilemma earlier and continues the theme. Royalty thus appears like a garment, to be put on or taken off, rather than an inherent, essential quality of the highest nobility. Hal's essential nobility, however, becomes evident even before he crosses swords with Hotspur. Already wounded, he rejects his father's entreaty to retire and insists on continuing the fight against the rebels. Moments later, he sees his father nearly vanquished by Douglas and comes directly to his rescue. For Henry, Hal has already redeemed his lost opinion by this action, which shows that Hal truly cares for him and does not long for his crown. But the greatest deed still remains unperformed, until the Prince and Hotspur at last meet and identify themselves.

It is the climax of the battle and of much else in the play. In their verbal exchanges before the duel as well as afterward, Hal shows himself both proud and courteous, while Hotspur is at best disdainful and overconfident, suggesting the earlier hubris and ill-temper that herald his tragic end. For Hotspur's death is in many respects the death of a tragic hero. A noble youth, princely in everything but title, misled by high motives, he makes a serious error (the tragic *hamartia*, in one of its definitions) that leads ultimately to his downfall and death. Beside him, feigning death but obscured from Hal's view, is the clown, plump Jack Falstaff, who listens as the prince first eulogizes

Hotspur and then himself. Hal might be thought of as the comic hero. Finally emerging as himself, he makes a garland for his head of all the "budding honors" that had decorated Hotspur's crest (V, iv, 71–77). He has used this day to best advantage, in that sense "redeeming time" (as Elizabethans would recognize), rather than squandering it in idleness or vain pursuits. Characteristically, as he lies dying, Hotspur remarks that he can better brook the loss of life than the loss of his "proud titles" that Hal has won from him. But even Hotspur recognizes that "thoughts the slaves of life, and life time's fool, / And time, that takes survey of all the world / Must have a stop" (V, iv, 80-82).

So it must, Hal recognizes, as he contemplates the immense distance between Hotspur's "ill-weaved ambition" and "two paces of the vilest earth" that soon will contain his corpse. Although fully capable of bestowing praise and courteous rites upon his fallen enemy, Hal is not now, anymore than previously, guilty of sentimentality or misdirected emotion. His eulogy over Falstaff fully reveals this aspect of his character. Changing his tone and punning appropriately, Hal reminds us that he is not so much in love with "vanity" as to miss the old knight excessively. Still, he "could have better spared a better man" (V, iv, 103). First and last, then, the Prince shows that he suffers from no illusions about himself, his friends, or the world. Valiant, sensitive, loyal to those things he holds most dear, he is above all clear-eyed and honest with himself in a world where these virtues, especially in combination, are scarce.

Hal also shows magnanimity, the greatest virtue in a prince, not only to Hotspur, but at the close to his brother, to Douglas, and to Falstaff. Whatever faults he has, fraternal jealousy is not one of them, and he is quick to recognize Prince John of Lancaster's valor on the field as well as Douglas's. Asking permission to dispose of Douglas, who has been captured in retreat, he fittingly gives the honor of releasing him, "ransomless and free," to Prince John (V, v, 28). Falstaff is another matter. At first astonished at seeing the fat knight alive and carrying Hotspur's body over his shoulder, Hal is further amazed at Falstaff's claim to have killed the warrior when both of them got up after Hal left them for dead. More taken by Falstaff's audacity than by his lie, and willing as ever to do him a favor, Hal agrees to help him get the credit for the deed by gilding his lie "with the happiest terms I have" (V, iv, 154).

Renouncing his own claim to killing Hotspur in order to help Falstaff is hardly chivalry on Hal's part. Chivalry is dead. In a sense, the wound that Falstaff inflicts upon Hotspur's thigh represents the final blow to chivalry by its chief antagonist. (Some critics interpret the action as a symbolic castration.) What survives, in Hal, will be a new kind of glory, neither the old glory of Hotspur, which he has surpassed, nor the somewhat spurious glory of the King, his father. As for Falstaff's "resurrection," we must await his further adventures in *The Second Part of King Henry the Fourth* to gauge fully its significance. He looks to be "either earl or duke" (V, iv, 139). He even promises that if he grows "great," he'll "grow less; for I'll purge, and leave sack, and live cleanly, as a nobleman should do" (V, iv, 159-61). Whether these are just promises on the order of his earlier resolutions to repent and reform remains to be seen.

Although Hotspur is dead and Worcester and Vernon are sentenced to immediate execution, the rebellion is not over. Northumberland, the Archbishop of York, Glendower, and Mortimer remain to be dealt with. No thought is given here to the crusade in the Holy Land, and Henry will die before he ever reaches there. Meanwhile, his son, Prince Hal, witnesses and learns much about the difficulties of ruling a kingdom. He learns to feel—as we do—the profound conflicts between the king as ruler and the king as a man. More than anything else, he comes to understand these problems, so that when finally he must put on his father's crown, he knows what choices he must make and how he must make them.

ANNOTATED BIBLIOGRAPHY

Barber, C.L. "From Ritual to Comedy: An Examination of *Henry IV*." In *English Stage Comedy: English Institute Essays*, edited by W.K. Wimsatt, Jr., pp. 22-51. New York: Columbia University Press, Reprint of 1954 edition. Also in Leonard F. Dean, ed. *Shakespeare: Modern Essays in Criticism*, rev. ed., pp. 144-66. New York: Oxford University Press, 1967.
Barber analyzes both parts of *Henry IV*, showing how Shakespeare fused two main traditions of saturnalian comedy: the clowning of the stage and the folly of holidays. Barber extends his analysis of Shakespearean comedy in *Shakespeare's Festive Comedy*. (Princeton: Princeton University Press, 1972.)

Bryant, J.A., Jr. "Prince Hal and the Ephesians." *The Sewanee Review* 67 (1959):204-19. Also in *Hippolyta's View: Some Christian Aspects of Shakespeare's Plays*. Lexington: University of Kentucky Press, 1961.
Bryant begins by showing how Hal's attempt to define for himself the proper sphere of honor provides a unifying force in *1 Henry IV*. Another unifying force is a "movement toward order—not just any order, but an order that is both politically acceptable and humane. . . ." A third, which Bryant develops in detail, is based on the allusion to St. Paul in Hal's first soliloquy—"Redeeming the time, because the days are evil"—so that a Christian order may be achieved as well as spiritual strength to combat evil. Hal's efforts to redeem Falstaff, however, are doomed.

Council, Norman. "Prince Hal: Mirror of Success." *Shakespeare Studies* 7 (1974):125-46.
Council refutes the quasi-Aristotelian paradigm of the theme of honor, as viewed by many critics, and offers a convincing discussion of Hal not as a mean between the extreme of honor (Hotspur) or its defect (Falstaff), but as a prince who uses honor for pragmatic purposes. Rather than Aristotle's *Ethics*, Council argues for Plato's description of man's tripartite soul in *The Republic*, Book IV, as a good philosophical scheme for the play.

Dorius, R.J., ed. *Twentieth Century Interpretations of* Henry IV, Part One. Englewood Cliffs, N.J.: Prentice-Hall, Inc., 1970.

A useful collection of essays and excerpts from a variety of critics and scholars exploring various aspects of the play, including a version of Barber's essay and parts of A.R. Humphrey's introduction to the Arden edition.

Saccio, Peter. *Shakespeare's English Kings: History, Chronical, and Drama.* New York: Oxford University Press, 1977.

Saccio analyzes Shakespeare's history plays in the context of actual historical events and in comparison with the principal sources in Holinshed's *Chronicles* and other Tudor histories.

Stewart, J.I. "The Birth and Death of Falstaff." In *Character and Motive in Shakespeare.* Studies in Shakespeare, No. 24. Brooklyn: Haskell House Publishers, Inc., 1977.

Stewart reviews major earlier criticism, including that of Morgann, Coleridge, Bradley, Stoll, and Dover Wilson, and focuses mainly on the genesis of Falstaff as a character in a play and on the interpretation of his rejection in Part II.

Wilson, John Dover. *The Fortunes of Falstaff.* London: Cambridge University Press, 1943.

Wilson offers a very full account of Falstaff and his relations to other characters. He emphasizes the morality pattern of the play and sees Falstaff in Part One as "Riot," or a Lord of Misrule, and Hal as a prodigal from chivalry, to which he returns.

SELF-TEST
Multiple-choice Questions
1. King Henry calls the Percys to court
   a. to congratulate them on their latest victories.
   b. to arrest them.
   c. to find out why they disobeyed him.
   d. to challenge them to battle.
2. All but one of the following phrases are metaphors used by Falstaff to describe himself and his cronies. Select the exception.
   a. ". . . squires of the night's body. . . ."
   b. ". . . dukes of dark corners. . . ."
   c. ". . . thieves of day's beauty. . . ."
   d. ". . . minions of the moon. . . ."
   e. ". . . gentlemen of the shade. . . ."
3. Which of the following does Hal agree to do in *1 Henry IV* to pull a prank on Falstaff?
   a. dress up as a tavern drawer
   b. disguise himself in Sir Thomas Erpingham's cloak
   c. cause Francis, the drawer, to run until he's ready to collapse
   d. participate in the Gad's Hill robbery
   e. assign Falstaff as commander of a ragtag squadron of troops
4. All but one of the following phrases are used to refer to Hotspur. Select the exception.
   a. ". . . the theme of honor's tongue. . . ."
   b. ". . . the very straightest plant. . . ."
   c. ". . . as wise as ancient lords. . . ."
   d. ". . . this all praised knight. . . ."
   e. ". . . Mars in swathling clothes. . . ."
5. Who is most concerned for Hotspur's personal welfare?
   a. his father Northumberland
   b. his uncle Worcester
   c. his wife Lady Percy
   d. Hotspur himself
6. Of the following characters, who is on Henry's side?
   a. Owen Glendower
   b. Edmund Mortimer
   c. Henry Percy
   d. Archbishop of York
   e. Walter Blunt
7. All but one of the following are setbacks experienced by the rebels. Select the exception.
   a. Northumberland is too ill to lead his army to the rebel camp.
   b. Owen Glendower cannot join the rebels at Shrewsbury at the agreed-upon date.
   c. An unnamed nobleman reveals the plans of the rebel to King Henry.
   d. The Earl of Douglas refuses to join the rebel forces.

8. Hotspur rationalizes the rebellion by telling Blunt each of the grievances listed below, except one. Which is *not* a grievance given?
   a. King Henry deposed Richard II.
   b. King Henry was responsible for Richard's death.
   c. King Henry levied heavy, unjust taxes.
   d. King Henry caused Mortimer, proclaimed heir to the crown, to remain captive in Wales.
   e. King Henry disgraced Hotspur after his victories against the Scots.
9. All but one of the following are ways in which Prince Hal demonstrates his valor, virtue, and courage. Select the exception.
   a. He offers to fight Hotspur in one-to-one combat to save bloodshed on either side.
   b. He fends off Douglas just in time to save his father's life.
   c. He insists on continuing the fight despite his bleeding wound.
   d. He frees Douglas, a foreigner, after the battle.
   e. He fights and slays Worcester on the battlefield.
10. Which of the following terms applies least well to Falstaff?
    a. coward
    b. braggart
    c. popinjay
    d. sharp-wit
    e. thief

Short-answer Essay Questions

1. Describe how the Percys justify the rebellion. Why did King Henry react to them as he did?
2. Describe Hal's attitude toward Falstaff and his other tavern friends. What, if anything, does he hope to gain from association with them?
3. Ned Poins persuades Hal to join the Gad's Hill plot by promising him fun with Falstaff's lies afterwards. Describe how well Poins predicted the events that follow the robbery.
4. Why do Northumberland, Glendower, and Mortimer fail to show up at Shrewsbury and join Hotspur and the others against Henry? Why does Hotspur decide to fight anyway, and what are the consequences?
5. Analyze Falstaff's soliloquy on "counterfeiting" in V, iv. How does this soliloquy epitomize Falstaff's cardinal attitudes and beliefs?

Questions for Reflection

1. Identify the qualities of Falstaff's prose and compare them with the qualities of blank verse passages, such as Hotspur's or Vernon's, that appear elsewhere. Besides the use of iambic pentameter, what are some of the differences and similarities between Shakespeare's verse and prose in this play? Are there any dramatic qualities appropriate to the one or the other form of discourse?
2. In the course of *1 Henry IV*, does Prince Hal mature, or does he only reveal his true qualities? If he matures, what are the major influences or experiences that help him? If he reveals his true qualities, describe what they are and explain why he has concealed them until nearly the end of the play.

3. Although women have just minor roles in *1 Henry IV*, what do they reveal about their position and men's attitudes toward them in Shakespeare's day? Do some of those same attitudes still exist today? Explain.
4. It is often said that in the Henriad Shakespeare attempted to define the qualities necessary for capable and just monarchical rule. From *1 Henry IV*, what qualities of kingship emerge that appear indispensable to a prince who would become "the mirror of a Christian king"? Does Henry IV demonstrate any of these qualities? Does Hal? Does Hotspur? Does Mortimer? Are any of these qualities indispensable for any other form of government?
5. Although chivalry in England may experience a mortal blow with the death of Hotspur, does every aspect of the code of honor die with him? What aspects remain? What new ones emerge? Are any still viable today, not only in politics and war, but in the conduct of other affairs, such as business, the professions (such as medicine, law), personal relationships?

ANSWER KEY

Answers to Multiple-choice Questions
1. c (I, i and iii)
2. b (I, ii)
3. d (I, ii)
4. c (a. I, i
   b. I, i
   d. III, ii
   e. III, ii)
5. c (II, iii)
6. e (evidence throughout the play)
7. d (a. IV, i
   b. IV, i
   c. II, iii)
8. c (IV, iii)
9. e (a. V, i
   b. V, iv
   c. V, iv
   d. V, v)
10. c (evidence throughout the play)

Suggested Answers to Short-answer Essay Questions
1. The Percys regard Henry IV as a usurper on the throne of England and feel that Edmund Mortimer, the Earl of March, has a better claim as the heir of Richard II. Moreover, they fear (Worcester especially) that Henry cannot forget how they helped him depose Richard and therefore will always mistrust them. Henry has become too powerful and does not, in his turn, defer to his former friends and supporters as he should. On his part, Henry feels that to keep order in the realm, he must assert the supremacy of the monarchy over the unruly northern nobles and other disruptive forces in the kingdom, like Owen Glendower in Wales.

2. That Hal enjoys Falstaff and the others who crowd around them at the Boar's Head Tavern cannot be denied. But Hal also sees through their fun and mischief and recognizes that he has other serious obligations that he will eventually have to assume. Meanwhile, as he tells us in his soliloquy at the end of I, ii, he will use these lowlife characters and his escapades with them to set off in striking contrast his "reformation" when the time comes for him to assert his regal character as Henry V. Hal sees through Falstaff's lies and pretensions to repentance but enjoys his wit and imagination, which provide more than just a holiday respite: They also help to sharpen Hal's perceptions and his understanding of all walks of life in the England he will someday rule as king.
3. Just as Poins predicted in I, ii, Falstaff enters the Boar's Head Tavern after the Gad's Hill robbery and, after calling everyone else a coward, begins a fantastic account of his own bravery in fighting off the counterattack by the men in the Kendal green. As his story grows, so do the numbers who attacked him, until he so exasperates the Prince that he tells what actually happened. The inconsistencies in his story (such as the utter darkness, but he could identify the color of men's clothes) do not faze Falstaff a bit and provide another source of merriment to the others who listen to him.
4. Northumberland sends word that he is sick and cannot trust the leadership of his troops in so important an engagement to anyone else. Glendower is warned by "prophecies" (IV, iv, 18) not to come in, and doubtless his son-in-law, Mortimer, follows his lead. But the cracks in the confederacy, shown earlier in III, i, probably account for this reluctance to join in at the crucial moment. As the champion of chivalry, Hotspur sees more glory in fighting, however outnumbered he is, than in heeding his uncle's prudent counsel to delay. In any event, the rebels do put up a good fight until Hotspur is killed and a rout begins, in which the valiant Douglas is captured and taken prisoner.
5. Although Falstaff at first uses "counterfeit" to describe his behavior when confronted by Douglas, he immediately rejects that term, since it does not truly describe him. A dead man is a counterfeit, he says, because he may look like a man but is not one, being dead. Falstaff is not dead; therefore, he is no "counterfeit" but truly alive and a man. To counterfeit dying to preserve life is not truly to be a counterfeit at all. He has exercised a proper "discretion," or choice, which in his view is a better quality of valor than reckless courage, which might have led to his death at Douglas's hands (as it did for Sir Walter Blunt, whose corpse Falstaff saw earlier on the battlefield). "Give me life," Falstaff proclaims (V, iii, 58); that is the important thing; honor is not much use when you are dead, nor is anything else. Since he is alive, he will take advantage of Hotspur's corpse, give him a fresh wound in his thigh, and claim he killed him.

The speech epitomizes Falstaff's chief concern for life at any cost. Just as he refused to grow old ("They hate us youth!"), he refuses to play the deadly game of chivalry that leads to many deaths on Shrewsbury Field. Pleasure is Falstaff's goal, not honor, and he will use every available means to promote his goal, including lying and making preposterous claims for himself. Language is malleable, and the meanings of words can be converted to best advantage by the exercise of wit, of which he has a superabundance as well as audacity to help it pay off.

THE SECOND PART OF KING HENRY THE FOURTH

INTRODUCTION TO THE PLAY

If you have been following the Henriad closely for the first time, *2 Henry IV* may strike you as something of an enigma. The clock seems to have been stopped or even turned back. True enough, the historical action of the play picks up chronologically where *1 Henry IV* ends—immediately following the battle at Shrewsbury (1403)—and covers the remaining years of Henry's reign until his death in 1413 and the subsequent elevation of Prince Hal to the throne as Henry V. Still, something's not quite right. The names and faces of a number of the major characters may be the same as in *1 Henry IV*, but somehow they also seem to be different. Prince Hal's character, for example, seems to have retrogressed. A major theme of *1 Henry IV* was Hal's apparent transformation from profligate into good, sober son and heroic prince. This process seemed concluded at Shrewsbury; yet in *2 Henry IV*, almost as though this transformation never took place, we are again treated to a Prince who is the disreputable pub-crawler of old, and who must mature again into responsibility before being reconciled with his father.

For some, a possible clue to this puzzle may be in the play's descriptive subtitle as printed in quarto in 1600: "With the humours of Sir Iohn Falstaffe, and swaggering Pistoll." This suggests that there were reasons other than historical enlightenment about the play's namesake that motivated the author. Elizabethan audiences had enjoyed Shakespeare's depiction of Prince Hal's early life as a highliving swain, and they had been captivated by the character and escapades of the fictitious Falstaff. In *2 Henry IV*, although expanding the role of the reigning monarch himself, Shakespeare nevertheless continues to allow Falstaff and Prince Hal to share the main spotlight, even promising Falstaff's reappearance in a subsequent play. The main plot involves the suppression of the Yorkist challenge to Henry IV's right to the throne and the (re)maturation of his son from wastrel to competent monarch. Falstaff's growing urgency for money to outfit himself luxuriously in the manner he feels befitting his new commission as leader of an expedition against the Yorkist insurgency, and his relationship to Prince Hal constitute the comic subplot.

The audience should be cautioned against dismissing the roisterous buffoonery as merely comic sidelight to the main action, for, as he did in Part I, Shakespeare has cleverly and inextricably interwoven the two. The realms of the court and of the tavern are sharply contrasted, and of the major characters only Hal and Falstaff belong to both. But Shakespeare ingeniously avoids permitting comic irrelevancies to interrupt the march of legend, and—because Prince Hal has to become Henry V by the end of the play—Shakespeare almost imperceptibly eases the Prince out of the comic realm of the taverns and into the historical realm of the court as the play progresses. At the same time, Shakespeare moves Falstaff in the other direction. The persistent mirth and revelry he and his sozzled companions engage in begins to wear thin and appear cheap. The bond between Hal and Falstaff is finally severed with Hal's coronation as Henry V and Falstaff's banishment from the court.

Those readers who have *not* been following the Henriad closely might do well to pause momentarily to review the action of the two preceding plays—*Richard II* and *1 Henry IV*—because of all the plays in the tetralogy, it is *2 Henry IV* that refers most frequently to events and personalities encountered in the other plays and that depends most heavily for comprehension and effectiveness on the audience's prior knowledge of events outside the play itself.

For one thing, almost a dozen characters from *1 Henry IV* are carried over into its sequel, including not only the expected historical persons such as Henry IV, Prince Hal, Prince John, and Archbishop Scroop, but also the fictional comic characters of Bardolph, Mistress Quickly, and, of course, Falstaff, whose role in the Henriad earned him a permanent niche in the English vocabulary. Knowing who these people are and their roles in the previous play is critical to an understanding of *2 Henry IV*.

For another, the audience for *2 Henry IV* is repeatedly thrown into the middle of events unresolved in the earlier two plays or into discussions of events that took place earlier. For example, *2 Henry IV* opens with the Earl of Northumberland receiving first false and then correct information on the outcome of the battle at Shrewsbury and the fate of his son, Hotspur. This mix-up and the ensuing discussion of the causes of and principal participants in the rebellion against Henry IV will be problematic to someone unfamiliar with the Byzantine politics of the preceding two plays. Similarly, in the first Falstaff scene of *2 Henry IV*, the conversation of the Lord Chief Justice and Falstaff assumes an audience that knows all about the Gad's Hill robbery in *1 Henry IV*.

Those of you who may have sensed some tension and discord between the two parts of *Henry IV* will find a friend in Stephen Booth, whose essay attempts to find a source for and to justify this feeling of unease. In his essay, "*Henry IV, Part Two* and the Aesthetics of Failure," Booth goes beyond the usual technique of analyzing plot, character, language, and other dramatic techniques and delves not only into the mind of the playwright himself but also into the collective minds both of the Elizabethan audiences for whom

Shakespeare originally wrote and of modern audiences. He rejects the usual excuse that modern and Elizabethan audiences were worlds apart in their understanding of the plays and concludes that Shakespeare deliberately set out to make audiences uncomfortable with *2 Henry IV*. Moreover, Booth feels that Shakespeare meant this play to fail as a sequel to Part I! Following Booth's reasoning in arriving at his startling conclusions makes fascinating reading, but be prepared to spend some time at it. His is not an easy essay. The arguments are sometimes subtle. Just as he is challenged to examine the motives of the playwright, so he challenges us to examine his logic; and just as he looks for answers in the reactions of audiences to a play, so he expects us to look for answers in our own reactions to the play and his essay. As with *2 Henry IV* itself, don't expect to be completely comfortable.

86   The Second Part of King Henry the Fourth

LESSON ASSIGNMENTS

In order to get the most out of the specially designed introductory material and to appreciate the unique qualities of the play itself, Stephen Booth strongly recommends that you prepare yourself in the following manner:
- View the television production. (Booth feels that your experiences with the two preceding plays of the Henriad provide you with adequate preparation for viewing *2 Henry IV*.)
- Read the synopsis of *2 Henry IV* in this guide.
- Read the text of *2 Henry IV*.
- Read "*Henry IV, Part Two* and the Aesthetics of Failure" by Stephen Booth in this guide.
- Complete the Self-test at the end of this lesson.

LEARNING OBJECTIVES

After completing the reading assignments and viewing the televised drama production, you should be able to:
1. Describe and contrast the interaction of the audience's expectations and the explicit roles and speeches of the following characters: Falstaff, Prince Hal, Henry IV, and Prince John.
2. Contrast the responses *the play* seems to expect with those that, in fact, it evokes with regard to the following characters: Falstaff, Prince Hal, Henry IV, and Prince John.
3. Identify the references in *2 Henry IV* to events and personalities in the other plays in the Henriad.
4. Describe the Gaultree Forest incident and indicate whether or how Shakespeare explains Prince John's treatment of the three rebel leaders.
5. Describe the similarities and differences between the reconciliations of Prince Hal with his father in *1 Henry IV* and *2 Henry IV*.
6. Identify some of the events and speeches that foreshadow the rejection of Falstaff by the newly crowned Henry V.

SYNOPSIS OF THE PLAY
ACT I

The Earl of NORTHUMBERLAND, claiming to be ill to avoid the Battle of Shrewsbury, learns that his son, Harry Percy (called HOTSPUR), has been killed and that a royal army is being sent against him. He vows to unite with the other rebels and attack the king.

In London, the LORD CHIEF JUSTICE denounces FALSTAFF as a thief and a corrupting influence on PRINCE HAL. Falstaff manages to wriggle out of this unpleasant encounter, and even asks the Lord Chief Justice for a loan.

Led by the ARCHBISHOP OF YORK, the northern rebels meet and decide they are strong enough to fight the King, even if Northumberland once again avoids battle.

ACT II

MISTRESS QUICKLY of the Boar's Head Tavern demands Falstaff's arrest for failing to repay the money he owes her. The Lord Chief Justice orders him to reimburse Mistress Quickly, but Falstaff takes the hostess aside and succeeds not only in having his debt canceled, but also in wheedling a second loan, a supper invitation, and the company of one of Mistress Quickly's girls, DOLL TEARSHEET.

News arrives that HENRY IV is ill, but Prince Hal explains to NED POINS that, given his prodigal background, he would be considered a hypocrite if he were publicly to show sorrow for his royal father. Learning that Falstaff is to dine with Mistress Quickly, Hal and Ned decide to disguise themselves as attendants and see Sir John "in his true colors."

In Northumberland's castle, his wife and daughter-in-law (Hotspur's widow) persuade him not to go to war against Henry IV, and to flee to Scotland.

Falstaff's convivial supper gathering at the tavern is disrupted by PISTOL, a swaggering but cowardly soldier, whom Falstaff eventually ejects. The Prince and Poins, in disguise, hear Falstaff describe the Prince in the most insulting terms. Irate, Hal and Poins confront him, but Falstaff grandly explains that he was being a true friend by preventing only the wicked from loving the Prince. Abruptly, Hal and Falstaff are called to arms against the rebels.

ACT III

Gravely ill and tormented by insomnia, Henry IV receives some good news: His enemies' armies are weakening.

Two old Justices, SHALLOW and SILENCE, meet their old friend Falstaff, who has arrived to recruit soldiers. He excuses those who can bribe their way out, and drafts the poorest and feeblest.

ACT IV

In the forest of Gaultree, the rebels learn that Northumberland has deserted them, and consider making peace. In parley with PRINCE JOHN OF LANCASTER, they are promised forgiveness on the condition that they disperse their armies. They do so, and are quickly arrested and taken off to be executed.

Arriving tardily at the battlefield, Falstaff captures a fleeing knight, then leaves for Justice Shallow's estate.

In the palace, the news of victory so excites King Henry that he has a seizure. Prince Hal returns and, mistaking his father's exhausted sleep for death, takes the crown with him from the room. The King awakes; finding the crown missing, he bitterly denounces Hal for being unable to wait for his death. Overcome, Prince Hal assures his father of his loyalty and love. Father and son are reconciled at last, and King Henry IV is carried to his deathbed.

ACT V

To curry favor with Falstaff because he is a link to Prince Hal, Justice Shallow organizes a dinner for him. Falstaff intends to borrow money from the gullible Shallow and plans to regale the Prince with stories about him.

News of Hal's kingship creates fear in the Lord Chief Justice, who once jailed him during his reckless youth. Hal reinstates the old official and reassures him that justice will prevail under his reign.

Falstaff's dinner with Justice Shallow is well underway when Pistol bursts in and joyously informs them that the King is dead and that Hal is to be crowned. Dazzled by his great prospects, Falstaff thunders off through the night to be at the new King's side.

Arriving in London in the nick of time, Falstaff stands in the most conspicuous spot as the coronation party passes by. Unable to ignore him, King Henry V publicly rejects Falstaff and banishes him with a pension. Falstaff reassures his friends that Hal will send for him in private, but he is quickly arrested by the Lord Chief Justice.

Prince John surveys the scene with satisfaction and foresees an expedition to France.

Henry IV, Part Two
and the Aesthetics of Failure

Stephen Booth

Henry IV, Part Two is a great play, a particularly powerful one, but one that is so variously and disturbingly unpleasant for its audience that, although one need not hesitate to call the play great, it is difficult and perhaps unjust to call it good. I will come back to justify and clarify the distinction I make between great and good. I want, however, to begin with—and use most of my allotted space on—justifying and clarifying the assertion that the play is unpleasant for its audience. The best way to start will be to examine and question the tempting notion that any element in a four-hundred-year-old play that disturbs or offends us would not have troubled its original audiences and will cease to trouble us once our viewpoint is corrected by prophylactic doses of historical information.

Anyone who has any experience at all of Shakespeare as presented in classrooms and in introductions to student texts knows the danger of forgetting that there are four hundred years between our values and assumptions and those of Shakespeare's contemporaries. I do not deny that danger, but I do suggest that it is often exaggerated and that the habit of mind we foster to forestall errors of chronological and cultural provincialism often invites us into intellectually convenient errors that result from a complementary danger—the danger of chalking off any Shakespearean effect that puzzles us to historical differences between twentieth-century mores and those of Shakespeare's time. The values and assumptions of the audiences Shakespeare wrote for were not identical with ours, but they appear to have been very, very similar. There is a great deal of clear documentary evidence for greater difference than I think existed in fact. Most such evidence is in political tracts, in sermons, in school books, and in other such sharply focused, purposefully persuasive statements of philosophic positions. Those positions were presented as self-evidently valid—presented over and over again from generation to generation during the sixteenth and seventeenth centuries. I do not have the space—and this is not the place—to present a full discussion of the matter. I hope it will suffice here to say that Renaissance tracts and sermons and books on political theory can give us the false impression that generally accepted Elizabethan ideas and ideals governed people's thinking about the topics to which those ideas and ideals pertain—can give us the false comfort of being able to say "Elizabethans thought 'X' about 'Y' " and then to argue away values and responses that contradict the particular governing principle to which we have appealed. In appealing to such principles, we need to remember that the reiteration of a moral, legal, or philosophical position advertises the fact that, though perhaps it should be, the position in question is not taken for granted by the populace on which it is so often pressed.

My reason for stressing the treacherousness of historical evidence that can seem to imply that a society is fanatic in the beliefs it most insistently promotes is that one can both feel and satisfy the urge to have an uncomplicated response to the characters and events of the Henry IV plays. For instance, reference to any one of a number of books of practical political and social philosophy (such as Thomas Elyot's *Book of the Governor* [published in 1531] and the Church of England's official "Homily against Disobedience and wilful Rebellion" [1563]), can seem to justify the very convenient belief that Shakespeare's contemporaries would have responded to, say, Prince John's "victory" over the rebels at Gaultree Forest (IV, i, ii) or the rejection of Falstaff by the new-crowned Henry V (V, v) in ways substantially different from ours. One can justly say that (like us), Elizabethans were familiar with, and ready to accept, the idea that action taken to ensure or preserve the health of the body politic is and should be exempt from evaluation by lesser standards of value. To say so, however, is not to say that in any given complicated case Elizabethans had any greater facility than we have for perceiving a particular action or event in one exclusive set of terms by virtue of which it is immune from the pull of considerations proper to other, lesser, but urgently active judgmental systems.

An Elizabethan audience might well have seen some justice in the proposition that, as outlaws, Archbishop Scroop and his faction have broken with the society they threaten and have thus surrendered their rights to the honorable treatment civilization gives to honorable men. I see, however, no historical reason to believe that the limited justice of that proposition carried more weight with Shakespeare's contempories than it does with us. "Policy"— the Elizabethan term for all kinds of cunning stratagem, craft, and purposeful deceit—was generally condemned; and so, in particular, was equivocation— Satan's own device (Macbeth refers to the "equivocation of the fiend / That lies like truth" [V, v, 43–44]). The first audiences to judge Prince John at Gaultree were made up of people as queasy about crafty use of technicalities as we are about legally innocent but morally guilty merchants who profit by contractual nuances hidden in small print; they were, for instance, raised on (rarely accurate and even more rarely just) horror stories about the equivocal tricks by which Jesuits tried to lead good English Protestants down the primrose road to Rome. Moreover, as he wrote the Gaultree scenes, Shakespeare passed up every opportunity to make his particular on-stage rebels feel villainous to his audience. He could have made Prince John's trick more palatable had he let his audience hear Scroop and company make unscrupulous plans of their own.

As to the rejection scene, an Elizabethan audience (like a modern one) must have seen that Hal's duty to his people requires that he purge himself, and thus the body politic, of Falstaff. There is, however, no reason whatever to believe that noble, public perceptions held exclusive sway in the minds of Elizabethans any more than they do in ours—no reason to doubt that Elizabethan audiences cringed as we cringe during the rejection scene. It is not, after all, so much the fact that Hal purges himself of Falstaff that offends audiences as the *way* he does it. After Falstaff has been publicly humiliated and led away by the Chief Justice's officers, Prince John refers to the incident as "this fair proceeding of the king's" (V, v, 98). The king's rejection speech does not strike modern audiences so, and there is no reason to think it struck Shakespeare's contemporaries so either. Hal's cold, distant, smug, priggish, uninterrupted and uninterruptible speech to Falstaff (V, v, 48–73) makes the new-crowned king sound like the sort of monstrous little demigod he specifically says he will not be in his treatment of his younger brothers (V, ii, 47–49, 57-58). The phrase "this fair proceeding" invites ironic snorts from audiences. The irony is presumably increased by the fact that Shakespeare puts the sanguine label "fair proceeding" in the mouth of the chill, perfidious prig who defeated the rebels with false words.

Only a critic fanatically determined to smooth away the moral and rhetorical rough spots in the play can believe that Shakespeare expected his play to be performed before an audience so devoted to the principles of proper kingship that its responses would be uncontaminated by the value western culture puts, and has traditionally put, on loyalty to friends, consideration for the feelings of others, and uncalculated warmth of manner.

To see the difference between the audience response the rejection scene evokes and the kind of response it could have evoked, consider the full text of Prince John's summary comment on it:

I like this fair proceeding of the king's.
He hath intent his wonted followers
Shall be very well provided for,
But all are banished till their conversations
Appear more wise and modest to the world.

(V, v, 98-102)

As Prince John presents the banishment it seems fair indeed. Notice the ordering of elements in the four-line sentence that makes up the body of the speech: The first clause focuses on the king's concern for the welfare of his former cronies; in the next clause, the word *but* introduces the morally responsible, disagreeable fact of banishment as a fact subordinate to the fact of the king's concern for his former followers; and, once acknowledged, the fact of banishment is immediately cradled on the other side by the hopeful final line and a half of the speech.

The rhetorical slant Prince John's summary gives to the banishment is, of course, emotionally unavailable to an audience that has seen and heard Falstaff's meeting with the new Hal, but the rhetoric of Prince John's speech presents a model for the rejection of Falstaff as Shakespeare *could* have written it. To make Hal's virtuous action feel virtuous to the audience, all Shakespeare would have needed to do is suggest that Hal regrets the pain it is his duty to inflict on Falstaff. Shakespeare could have given Hal a soliloquy or tacked a reference to his impending painful sacrifice into the speech to his brothers in V, ii (44–61), or even had him express some regret directly to Falstaff in the course of the rejection speech. Shakespeare could surely have ensured some kindly feeling for Hal from the audience by giving his provision for Falstaff's financial security a fraction of the prominence it gets in Prince John's speech—gets after the audience's affection for Hal has been irrevocably lost. Instead, however, Shakespeare buries Hal's charity among decrees that are harsh and harshly phrased, gives a sanctimonious rather than a humane reason for the pension, and reports the fact of the pension to us in a syntactic construction ("For competence of life I will allow you" [V, v, 67]), so mushy and vague that it is no wonder that audiences often leave the theater without even noticing that Hal has provided Falstaff with a pension.

Not only does Shakespeare miss chances to soften our responses to Hal, he carefully throws away the negative rhetorical energy he has generated in his audience's relationship to Falstaff. Falstaff, whose essential corruption has been generally more evident in Part Two than it was in Part One, gets the comeuppance we have recently seen him court by his confident boasting ("the laws of England are at my commandment" [V, iii, 133]); Shakespeare could have made our experience of the rejection scene easier for us if it had included a reminder of Falstaff's plans for a future as the privileged bully he believes himself now licensed to be. Falstaff is raucous and pathetically confident as he awaits the coronation procession, but he does nothing to remind us of the threat he plans to pose to other people.

All in all, Shakespeare seems to have worked hard at making sure that, though an audience *sees* the virtue and moral necessity of the separation of Hal and Falstaff, it cannot *feel* it to be so.

My argument for the probability that twentiety-century responses to *2 Henry IV* are not anachronisms is now as full as I can make it here. Henceforth, availing themselves of a liberty I hope is justified by the case I have sketched out in the preceding paragraphs, my speculative descriptions of responses to *2 Henry IV* will, when it is just to do so, use the terms "the audience," "we," and "us" to refer without distinction to Shakespeare's audiences in his own time, ours, and times intervening.

I want now to move on to a quite different fact of *2 Henry IV* by which an audience's experience of it is and, I think, must always have been not only unsatisfactory but disquietingly so: The play presents itself as a diminished shadow of its predecessor. *2 Henry IV* consistently makes and breaks promises to be the kind of sequel that *Godfather II, Rocky II*, and the current series of cookie-cutter *Airport* sequels are—sequels that promise to be, and work at being, new incarnations of their hugely popular originals—new incarnations that give us variations on what pleased us the first time.

As Allan Chester says in his introduction to the Pelican text of *2 Henry IV*, there has been a lot of scholarly speculation and dispute about whether the two Henry IV plays are two halves of a planned, artistically coherent whole or the result of one or another kind of accident; but, whatever the play's inception may have been, there is no denying that *2 Henry IV* seems like a flat, muted echo of *1 Henry IV*. One can try—and critics have indeed tried—to look at the play in its own terms as an independent entity—"not" (in David Young's words), "merely as a sequel but a full-fledged member of the canon and a separate and unified work of art." The play, however, will not cooperate with critical efforts to alleviate the bad effects of its unsuccessful sibling rivalry with Part One. The play is sprinkled with insistent references to events in Part One—particularly events in the Falstaff story, which is entirely Shakespeare's creation (reference to the events at Gad's Hill or to the big tavern scene in *1 Henry IV* cannot be accounted for as necessities of the continuity of dramatized chronicle).

Moreover, and more important, many scenes *insist* on their identities as echoes of similar scenes in *1 Henry IV*. Most important, the echoing scenes come just close enough to duplicating the success of their originals that audiences find themselves constantly trying to, failing to, and feeling somehow guilty in failing to respond as they did in Part One. I base the assertion about trying, failing, and feeling guilty on the de facto testimony innate in the many just but often shrill, suspiciously eager, and usually defensive critical assertions that, for example, Falstaff is still funny and that such things as Shallow and Silence as comic creations and the relationship of Falstaff and Doll are as rich and satisfying as anything in Part One.

As an example of a scene that not only seems designed to duplicate the effects of an original in Part One but also comes close to convincing us that we should find it charming and innocent in the way its elder twin was charming and innocent, consider II, ii, Prince Hal's first scene in Part Two. The first topic of that scene is the first topic of Hal's first scene in Part One (I, ii): the discrepancy between his high, responsible station and the life of frivolity and low company he actually leads. And, as the last topic of conversation in I, ii of Part One was Poins's scheme to trick Falstaff during the robbery at Gad's Hill, this corresponding scene in Part Two concludes with Poins's plans for another practical joke on Falstaff. The spirit of this scene is not only ostensibly but ostentatiously the spirit of the comparable scene in *1 Henry IV*. The opening lines establish a tone—a tone from which the scene cannot be said ever to lapse: the bantering tone of friends who exercise their mutual affection by playfully mocking each other and themselves:

> PRINCE *Before God, I am exceeding weary.*
> POINS *Is't come to that? I had thought weariness durst not have attached one of so high blood.*
> PRINCE *Faith, it does me, though it discolors the complexion of my greatness to acknowledge it. Doth it not show vilely in me to desire small beer?*
>
> (II, ii, 1–6)

Presumably the tone established in Poins's first line is immediately recognized as benign, and governs the audience's response to the succeeding badinage, but the scene will not let us be easy about giving the responses it so obviously demands. When Hal picks up on Poins's mock surprise, he continues in Poins's vein ("Doth it not show vilely in me to desire small beer?"); his own mock surprise pretends to respond to the absurd notion that a great man who is thirsty is unlikely to want to quench his thirst with any drink but one that is strong and expensive. When Hal mentions small beer, his reference—coming as it does upon his declaration of weariness—is literal: he refers to thin beer of low alcoholic content. But "small beer" was already a proverbial phrase meaning "trivial things," "matters of no consequence," and in the course of Poins's response ("Why, a prince should not be so loosely studied as to remember so weak a composition" [II, ii, 7–8]), and Hal's response to that (". . . by my troth, I do now remember the poor creature small beer" [II, ii, 10–11]), the metaphoric sense emerges. When Hal's speech drifts from his desire for a nonglamorous beverage to Poins as a person who is "small beer," the transition is neither so abrupt nor so gratuitously callous as it would be if it were not buoyed by the play between the literal and metaphoric senses of "small beer":

> POINS *Why, a prince should not be so loosely studied as to remember so weak a composition.*
> PRINCE *Belike, then, my appetite was not princely got, for, by my troth, I do now remember the poor creature, small beer. But indeed these humble considerations make me out of love with my greatness. What a disgrace is it to me to remember thy name! Or to know thy face to-morrow! Or to make note how many pair of silk stockings thou hast . . .*
>
> (II, ii, 7–15)

However, no commentator—either by demonstrating the real though meager wit of the play on "small beer" or by insisting on the undeniable fact that Hal is only joking and takes his cue from Poins—can deny that the transition from small beer to Poins as mere "small beer" *is* gratuitous and *is* callous.

The contrast between Hal's behavior and companions and those proper to a prince is, as I said earlier, also a topic of the corresponding scene in *1 Henry IV*; moreover, that scene, I, ii, concludes with the soliloquy in which, in effect, Hal says that his present identity as a playboy is as purely a disguise as the one he plans at Gad's Hill. The soliloquy presents his calculating and well-calculated long-range plans to exploit his imminent reformation rhetorically. The speech is not and can never have been easy to take, but Shakespeare makes it easier for us than it would be if he had not isolated our experience of the cold and purposeful "real" Prince Henry in the soliloquy, where it has less power to discolor the complexion of the good old boy Hal is in the body of the scene.

Throughout *1 Henry IV* Shakespeare keeps us aware of Hal's two identities and the need for the warm, lovable one to fall before the cold, responsible, efficient one. The necessary and necessarily painful consequences of that defeat are brought home to us in isolated flashes, but most of the time Shakespeare so presents the ideas, ideals, and events of Part One that we can exercise valid but conflicting allegiances without mental difficulty; he lets us espouse Hal's private virtues and his public ones without facing and having to wrestle with the fact that in the situation described in the play they are incompatible. Exactly the opposite is true in Part Two, and the contrast between I, ii of *1 Henry IV* and its counterpart in *2 Henry IV* demonstrates the fact. In the first play Falstaff introduces the topic of Hal's rank and harps on it throughout the scene, but Hal himself ignores his high birth and station throughout his conversations with Falstaff and Poins and takes the matter up only in the isolation of the closing soliloquy. In the comparable scene of Part Two the subject of Hal's "high blood" is introduced by Poins, but Hal refuses to let the topic drop; his consciousness of hierarchical superiority to Poins and Poins's style of life is a persistent and disturbing fact of the whole scene.

Hal jokingly says that it is low of him to know the petty details of Poins's daily life; however, he demonstrates not only that he knows all about the economy of Poins's wardrobe but that he takes pleasure in documenting Poins's genteel poverty and mocking him for it. Hal's values and sense of proportion seem wrong.

In supporting the assertion that *2 Henry IV* often feels like *1 Henry IV* gone sour, I chose to talk about II, ii because elements in it suggest that Shakespeare knew exactly what he was doing and did so on purpose. For instance, the topic of appropriate, inappropriate, feigned, and unfeigned responses is one that the characters themselves discuss (II, ii, 27–63). Also consider Poins's scornful comment (II, ii, 101–7) on Falstaff's ostentation about his status as a knight—a comment altogether pertinent to the audience's experience of the status-conscious Prince Hal, but a comment so superfluous to the business of getting Falstaff's letter read out for the audience that it is commonly cut in performance. Poins makes fun of royalty's distant relatives not so much for their vanity as for the contortions they perform in order to advertise their distinction. Prince Hal is no way comparable to the distant kin of royalty, but the reported conversational tactics of the poor relations Poins describes are only exaggerated versions of those by which Hal persistently leads conversation back to the matter of his own birth and station.

Even in its last painful moments the play activates an audience's longing for the lost theatrical joys of *1 Henry IV.* Consider these lines from the rejection speech:

> *Know the grave doth gape*
> *For thee thrice wider than for other men.*
> *Reply not to me with a fool-born jest.*
>
> (V, v, 54–56)

The sentence beginning "Reply not" responds to Falstaff's silent offer to respond to the sentence about the gaping grave. The sentence beginning "Reply not" acts as stage directions do in modern plays; it instructs the actor playing Falstaff that he is to open his mouth or otherwise signal that he is about to offer a rejoinder, one that an audience would like to hear. An audience to *2 Henry IV* remembers the fun it had when Falstaff turned aside or rose above similar insults in Part One. In this echo of that play the boon companions Hal and Falstaff have only once before been on stage together and then (in the sequence set off by "No abuse . . . I dispraised him before the wicked" [II, iv, 298 ff.]), gave the audience only a taste of their skill in comic thrust and chop-logic parry.

In the preceding pages I have not only argued that *2 Henry IV* is variously unpleasant and unsatisfying for its audiences; I have also presented evidence that suggests that Shakespeare set out purposefully to write a play that would fail to please and would seem to fail because its author could not quite achieve the effects he wanted. The suggestion that a great artist set out to fail is bizarre—and infinitely more convenient and ingenious than the argument of critics who try to rescue the play by assuring us that our responses are historically invalid. Yet—although I recommend that you treat the notion with great suspicion, and although I remain suspicious of it myself—I do indeed suggest that *2 Henry IV* might be as it is for tactical reasons.

Traces of evidence that Shakespeare knew he was giving his audience a hard time in *2 Henry IV* and meant to do so are interesting to a student of Shakespeare (the author) rather than of "Shakespeare" (the plays—in this instance one play, *2 Henry IV*). Such traces are also comforting to me as advocate for criticism that accepts audience discomfort as a fact of *2 Henry IV.* If, however, my sense of an audience's plight during the play is accurate, and if my notion is valid that the real experience of audiences *as* audiences reflects the discomfort of characters who have heard the chimes at midnight and cannot come again to yesterday, what I say is no more true if Shakespeare meant to achieve that effect—and would be no less true if the failures of *2 Henry IV* could be demonstrated to be accidental (if, for example, somebody found a lost letter from Shakespeare saying that he set out to duplicate the successes of *1 Henry IV* but couldn't bring them off a second time). Neither knowledge of Shakespeare's intentions in echoing Part One in Part Two—knowledge we are unlikely ever to get—nor speculative arguments about his intentions are in any way relevant to the effects the play actually has on audiences. That is obvious. I want only to assure you that, though I am considering two related issues here, I know as well as you do that my speculative account of the way *2 Henry IV* acts upon its audience and my more purely speculative case for Shakespeare's purposeful failure to please are two distinct matters; I do not intend the second as support for the first.

If that is understood, I can go on.

In frustrating its audience's expectations, in casually accommodating elements and events that are disturbingly difficult to reconcile with their surroundings, and in foregoing rather obvious literary strategies for keeping its audience comfortable, *2 Henry IV* is unusual among Shakespeare's plays *only* in degree. Throughout his career—from *Love's Labor's Lost* (which abruptly balks at reaching the comic conclusion it promises, and in which characters in the fiction comment on the audience's surprise) all the way to *The Tempest*—Shakespeare appears to have been fascinated by audiences' generically or locally derived expectations and assumptions and by the theatrical energy to be had from playing his play off against the one the audience manufactures and tries to see. I suggest that *2 Henry IV* is merely the most perverse and vexing of Shakespeare's many experiments with perversity. He regularly troubled his audience's equilibrium by introducing generically uncomfortable elements into plays that do not acknowledge that anything disturbing at all happened. What makes the Gaultree incident so difficult for an audience is the fact that no one *inside* the play condemns it or justifies it or recognizes the need to do one or the other. The play presents the incident as if it expected us to accept John's trick as ordinary—as morally regular as any other military tactic. Similarly, our biggest difficulty in the rejection scene derives from the play's apparent expectation that our response to it will be as sanguine and uncomplicated as Prince John's. The play keeps setting up a conflict between what we think during a scene and what we feel we ought to think. The dilemmas I am talking about are merely theatrical—ultimately trivial in, and peripheral to, our lives outside the theater, lives in which a few hours in the theater are only a diversion—but, in their scale, they are powerful and—being of our real experience, our experience of being an audience to a play—they are *real* dilemmas.

Shakespeare creates similar but less intense little dilemmas all the way through his career. Consider the following typical examples from plays you are seeing this year. (Any one thing in the following list could be chalked up to accident or to a lapse in Shakespeare's dramatic proficiency, but—since there are similar examples in every single Shakespeare play—it is worth considering the probability that they are deliberate.) In I, v of *Hamlet*, Hamlet puts on his "antic disposition" fifty-odd lines before he announces his plan to do so; we are left to feel silly for not knowing what we had no way of knowing. In *Twelfth Night*, Shakespeare presents us with Malvolio—a stick-figure comic villain who unexpectedly takes on a human dimension by which it becomes difficult to follow the play's continuing requirement that he be considered a farce creature no more entitled to sympathy than Cinderella's stepsisters. At the end of the same play the gratuitous cruelty of Toby's unexpected, unexplained last line suddenly upsets our sense of him and his relationship with Andrew, who has offered to help him: "Will you help? An ass-head and a coxcomb and a knave, a thin-faced knave, a gull?" (V, i, 198–99). At the end of *The Tempest* everyone who has done, or tried to do, injury to Prospero has a speech of repentance—except the prime villain: The wicked brother who overthrew Prospero neither remarks on Prospero's charity nor acknowledges any sense whatever of his guilt; after Prospero forgives him, the only line Antonio speaks is a casual wisecrack about Caliban's fishlike appearance. And Shakespeare creates a Prospero whose manner and incidental behavior are petulant, cruel, unjust, and tyrannical—are perfectly at odds with the superbenign, supercharitable being we know him to be and that all the significant events of the plot prove him to be.

A more complex and more immediately relevant example of Shakespeare's genuine but constructive perversity in dealing with his audience and in wantonly ignoring chances to please it is the truly remarkable way he treated his raw materials in *1 Henry IV*. Those materials dictate that the play lead to a climax in Hal's sudden reformation at Shrewsbury—his revelation as the man who will be the heroic Henry V. In the play the epiphany at Shrewsbury surprises Hal's fellow characters but can never have surprised audiences, which—well acquainted with the legends of Henry the Fifth—are as ready to be surprised by the new Hal as a movie audience is when things go badly for General Custer at the Little Bighorn.

The audience's foreknowledge of the surprise in store for Hal's contemporaries gives Shakespeare all the advantages of a central character of the King David type. We, the audience, delight in our exclusive knowledge that the foolhardy shepherd boy really *is* a match for Goliath. This particular, great, true, and easily achieved pleasure is the mainspring of countless biographical films of the 1930s and 1940s: *We* don't laugh at the boys for letting a good bicycle business deteriorate; we have reason to believe that a heavier-than-air vehicle *can* fly. This is a rich pleasure that Shakespeare later offers in all its high-calorie crudeness in the scenes before Agincourt.

In Hal—wastrel prince and hero-king—Shakespeare has a character whom *only* Shakespeare, a superhuman and superhumanly perverse writer, could make other than the instant and perfect darling of an audience. Shakespeare denies us any emotionally satisfying opportunity to exercise our inside knowledge of Hal's heroic future between the "night-tripping fairy" speech in I, i (78–91) and the contemptuous lines with which Hotspur introduces Vernon's "feathered Mercury" speech (IV, i, 94–97). Shakespeare also takes pains to disperse among the other characters all the attractions readily available to a character of Hal's literary type: the charm of youthful rashness and idiosyncrasy is lavished upon Hotspur and denied to Hal; the love that audiences bear to resourceful rascals and winsome rioters is diverted to Falstaff—who also bests Hal in their continuing contest of wit, a contest where the prize is the affection of the audience.

The historical prejudice we brought with us into the theater makes Hal our hero, but we cannot love him. Shakespeare's Hal is like Milton's God: We want to love him because we know he deserves the love we do not feel for him. By denying us the easy pleasure inherent in our foreknowledge of Hal's surprising reformation, Shakespeare manages to make it surprise us. What he does is substitute a real literary surprise for the substantial one that, because of our historical vantage point, we cannot share. Audiences cannot scorn Hal in the way his contemporaries did, but they do scorn him in theatrical terms, underrating him *as a character*—a source of pleasure, an object for their attention, admiration, and affection. At Shrewsbury, Shakespeare suddenly makes it possible for our emotions to sustain the judgment of history; Hal becomes the single object both of our intellectually granted respect and of our rhetorically earned and emotionally paid admiration. The miraculous transformation in our feeling for Hal as a theatrical character substitutes for the unavailable sense of wonder at his moral transformation.

I presented the foregoing examples to demonstrate that Shakespeare commonly takes risks with his audience's tolerance, and that he sees and uses the rhetorical potential available in friction between what an audience wants and expects and what it gets; with the last example I sought both to demonstrate precedent in Shakespeare for failure to exploit obvious, theatrically inviting tactics for satisfying an audience and to show you how an audience's experience of a play *as play* can inform its experience of, and responses to, the people and events the play presents. I do not, of course, mean to equate the minor uneasiness of an audience unable to warm to Hal through most of Part One with the more urgent and pervasive uneasiness of an audience to Part Two. However, in the next play—the play in which we are invited to delight in the virtuous exploits of Henry V at Agincourt—Shakespeare flirts with failure almost as perversely, almost as daringly, and at least as blatantly as he does in *2 Henry IV*. As you will see when you get to it, *Henry V* demands that we adore its hero, but Shakespeare persistently and meticulously undercuts each of his best efforts to secure, and make us secure in, our adoration (pay particular attention to the Chorus's introductions and their pertinence to the scenes that immediately follow them). There are, throughout the Henriad, but particularly in the last two plays, distinct signs that Shakespeare seeks to make rhetorical use of calculated audience awareness of the plays' inadequacy to do what they signal a desire to do. The readiest example is the first speech of *Henry V*: the grossest may be the whole of *2 Henry IV*.

It is now reasonable to inquire what Shakespeare achieved by working against his audience's, and thus his own, apparent interests in *2 Henry IV*—to inquire what he achieved by failing. To begin with, it is altogether reasonable to note the propriety of this play's weariness *as play* to the variously exhausted characters it presents. The play is full of tired old men, and the first thing Prince Hal says in *2 Henry IV* is that he is exceedingly weary. The last of the new major characters introduced in the play is Justice Shallow, who spends his time remembering "with advantages" the deeds of his youth. Similarly, the breaking of promises that were never quite made is also a topic of this play that variously promises to be what it fails to be. The issue is most urgently apparent in the equivocation at Gaultree, but it pertains also to Northumberland's failure to support his allies and to the disappointment of Falstaff's happy (and the Lord Chief Justice's unhappy) expectations about the new regime. When the new-crowned Henry V says "Presume not that I am the thing I was" (V, v, 57), he says to Falstaff what *2 Henry IV* has been saying about itself all the way through.

It is also reasonable to point out that, as this play—which starts out focused on the events of the Battle of Shrewsbury, and which then behaves as if Prince Hal's epiphany at Shrewsbury had never occurred—leisurely retraces a progress already completed, an audience is inevitably willing the play to hurry up and get where it is going. We know where this play is going. We know both its destinations: the re-revelation of Hal as the Henry V that will be, and a final break with Falstaff. Thus, in objecting to one disturbing fact of the play we are its accomplices in another. In fact we are—and have been since we came into the theater to see Prince Hal surprise everybody by reforming—generally and necessarily implicated in the rejection of Falstaff. We have endorsed—and have reveled in our historically confirmed faith in— every one of Hal's reassurances to his father.

At this point it would be easy, comfortable, reasonable, and just to put forward the conclusion that Shakespeare's dramatic tactics in *2 Henry IV* present us an onomatopoeia-like reflection of the disturbing truths embodied in the situations and actions of the characters: Shakespeare's play—what he *wrote*—is to what he writes *about* rather as a line of gurgling verse describing a gurgling brook is to the brook it describes. It would be easy, comfortable, reasonable, and wrongheaded to put forth a companion conclusion: that, in evoking dissatisfaction with the kinds of scenes, actions, and characters that delighted us when we were younger, the play's failures lead us into an emotional commitment to the wisdom and deep personal heroism of apparently, but only apparently, mean-spirited actions like Hal's when he rejects Falstaff. The injustice of the second hypothetical conclusion is transparent: if the experience of following this play has such edifying potential, how does it happen that potential is not realized in the theater and is not apparent at all except as it emerges from a carefully managed critical essay?

I do, however, insist that *2 Henry IV* is a great play, great by virtue of the power the play has as a result of the mental discomforts it generates in its audience. In *2 Henry IV* Shakespeare could have settled for merely demonstrating the painful necessities incumbent upon human beings who must act on the basis of one set of values and must therefore violate others that, if less persuasive, are humanly more demanding. Such a demonstration would have sat well with an audience, but would have lacked the genuine power *2 Henry IV* has. By genuine power I mean power as a real, albeit merely theatrical, experience beyond the vicarious experience of painful decisions by characters we watch and hear.

Given that account of the play and a culture as ready as ours is to assume that anything we do not like must be good for us, one might be drawn to say that *2 Henry IV* is not only a great play (one with such power to evoke such powerful responses) by a great and daring writer in full control and at the top of his form, but also a good one. I distinguish great and good because the idea of a good play includes its success as a theatrical commodity pleasurable and satisfying to its audience. If we accede to the hypothesis that in *2 Henry IV* Shakespeare purposefully sacrificed his ego and (as he more palpably did when he broke his own promise and left Falstaff out of *Henry V*) sacrificed the pleasure of his audience to some goal "higher" (or at least more complex and more difficult to achieve), we should not therefore ask ourselves to make our judgment neat by praising a disappointing play on the grounds that it succeeds in being disappointing. Parody aside, there is no such thing as an imitation bad play; the counterfeit is inevitably real. Shakespeare's *tactic* succeeds (if, indeed, it is a tactic and not a sudden lapse in skill), but, like the tactic whereby one treats of ennui by engendering it in one's audience, it is misconceived. Shakespeare elsewhere experiments successfully with frustrating audiences' dramatic expectations and withholding their moral and aesthetic perquisites, but in *2 Henry IV*, although he may succeed in the perverse rhetorical purposes I propose, he does not succeed in making his audience like it. I admire *2 Henry IV* and, obviously, I like thinking about it, but I do not *like* it—do not like it as I like *1 Henry IV*, *Hamlet*, and chocolate bars. Do you? (In answering that question, do not let yourselves be led astray by reason.)

ANNOTATED BIBLIOGRAPHY

Humphresy, Arthur R. "Introduction." In *The Second Part of King Henry IV*. Arden Shakespeare Series. London: Methuen Inc., 1966. (New York: Barnes and Noble Books, 1966.)

In eighty-three pages, and under ten main headings (Publication, Date, Extent of Revision, Relationship to *1 Henry IV*, Sources, Themes, Falstaff, The Rejection, Style,

The Text), Humphresy presents the scholarly essentials necessary as a starting point for informed study of the play.

Hunter, G.K. "*Henry IV* and the Elizabethan Two-Part Play." *Review of English Studies* New Series V, 19 (1954):236–48.

As its title suggests, the essay considers the genre to which the Henry IV plays belong; Hunter displays the "diptych-unity" of two-part plays by Marlowe, Marston, and Chapman; a long note provides a useful account of two-part plays in which the relation of parts is dissimilar to that of the Henry IV plays.

Jorgensen, Paul A. "The 'Dastardly Treachery' of Prince John of Lancaster." *PMLA* 76 (1961):488–92.

Jorgensen presents an illuminating, nonpolemic survey of trends in Elizabethan attitudes toward, and experience of, "the breach of the lawe of Armes, of treachery and murther that comes thereby."

Young, David P., ed. *Twentieth Century Interpretations of* Henry IV, Part Two. Englewood Cliffs, N.J.: Prentice-Hall, 1968.

This work contains substantial essays by six influential critics and short excerpts from longer works by seven others. In a brief but full introduction to the collection, Young provides a clear and efficient account of the issues that have most concerned people who have commented on *2 Henry IV*. Among the six essays, students will do well to start with L.C. Knights's "Time's Subject: The Sonnets and *King Henry IV, Part II*" (which, though its title sounds specialized, presents a wise, humane, and restrained account of the play) and C.L. Barber's simultaneously sophisticated and straightforward "The Trial of Carnival in *Part Two*." Among the shorter pieces, note A.P. Rossiter's "Ambivalence: The Dialectic of the Histories"—a crisp and persuasive plea against ideological neatness achieved at the cost of common sense and the truth of the play.

SELF-TEST

Multiple-choice Questions
1. Which of the following characters in *2 Henry IV* did NOT appear in the text of *1 Henry IV*?
   a. Lord Bardolph
   b. Lord Chief Justice
   c. the Archbishop of York
   d. Pistol
   e. Lady Percy
   f. Doll Tearsheet
   g. Prince John
   h. the Earl of Northumberland
2. At the beginning, *2 Henry IV* is concerned with
   a. lies.
   b. vice.
   c. rumors.
   d. virtue.
3. How does Prince John capture the rebels?
   a. He sneaks into their camp and kidnaps them.
   b. He harshly defeats them on the battlefield.
   c. He deceives them in the parley, then arrests them.
   d. He pretends to join them, then betrays them.
   e. He invites them to parley, then suddenly attacks.
4. How does the King react when Prince Hal tries on the crown while he (the King) is still alive?
   a. He swells with fatherly pride.
   b. He is angered.
   c. He is indifferent.
   d. He pretends not to notice.
   e. He laughs with delight.
5. Henry's rejections of Falstaff can best be described as
   a. a warm parting between two old friends.
   b. an angry debate.
   c. a cold, harsh denial.
   d. a sentimental but necessary farewell.
6. It had been long prophesied that Henry IV would die in
   a. disgrace.
   b. the Palace at Westminster.
   c. Gloucestershire.
   d. the year 1413.
   e. Jerusalem.
7. Why doesn't Prince Hal show grief at his father's illness?
   a. He claims that he does not truly love his father.
   b. He feels that he would be looked upon as a hypocrite if he did.
   c. He feels his father is too great a man to die suddenly.
   d. He doesn't feel that his father is all that sick.
   e. He says he plans to rush in at the last minute so he'll look more concerned.

8. In *2 Henry IV*, Falstaff borrows money from two characters and tries to borrow from a third. The three are
   a. Mistress Quickly, Bardolph, and Silence.
   b. the Lord Chief Justice, Silence, and Mistress Quickly.
   c. Bardolph, Silence, and Shallow.
   d. Silence, the Lord Chief Justice, and Bardolph.
   e. Mistress Quickly, Shallow, and the Lord Chief Justice.
9. What reason did Prince Hal give for trying on King Henry's crown?
   a. He wanted to see if it would fit his head.
   b. He wanted to get the feeling of "exhilaration and pride" that comes with wearing the crown.
   c. He wanted to challenge it because it had "murdered" his father.
   d. He wanted to look at himself in the mirror with it on to see how he would appear as king to his subjects.
   e. He explained that since his father was almost dead, the crown would soon be his anyway.
10. How does Falstaff react to Henry's rejection of him?
    a. He is shocked and curses until he realizes he will get a pension.
    b. He is taken aback but rationalizes that the King will secretly send for him later.
    c. He becomes very angry and disillusioned and predicts his own death.
    d. He becomes sad and cries at the thought of never seeing the "sweet prince" again.
    e. He laughs it off and rationalizes away the rejection, although it is obvious that he is inwardly sad.

Short-answer Essay Questions

1. Shakespeare includes some characters who have no immediately obvious dramatic function. Can you see any functions that the following characters serve—functions that might explain why Shakespeare bothered to put them in his play?
   (a) Falstaff's Page
   (b) Davy
   (c) The three grooms who have a line each at the beginning of V, v (the last scene)

2. Shakespeare also includes whole scenes that are neither necessary to telling the story, useful for establishing character, nor particularly entertaining. Such scenes are often cut in performance. Give some reason for retaining the scene in which the Beadle arrests Doll and Mistress Quickly (V, iv).

3. Shakespeare's company appears not only to have doubled parts regularly but to have done so in ways that ensured that the best actors got to do as much as possible—were not, for example, wasted on demanding characters who appear only in the first parts or only in the last parts of plays. Rumor, Northumberland, and Poins appear only in the early acts of *2 Henry IV*. Can you suggest later assignments for the actors who played those parts—assignments comparable in prominence to those they had earlier, and assignments whereby the particulars of the *production* of the play might underscore likenesses and contrasts between pairs of characters?

4. Comment on the pertinence of the last speech of the play (Prince John's speech about the coming wars in France), and the Epilogue to the Induction spoken by Rumor.

Questions for Reflection

1. A lot of sharply contrasted characters, actions, and situations in *2 Henry IV* are also alike (for instance, the Lord Chief Justice and Shallow are both judges; both II, iii and II, iv present old men who are about to go off to war and whom we see in conversation with women; Lord Bardolph and Falstaff's crony both have the same name). What are the effects of such incidental likenesses and differences?
2. Consider the order in which events are presented and characters introduced. What effect has it on the play that the title character does not appear until its tenth scene (III, i)? What effect results from the juxtaposition of the recruiting scene (III, ii) and the Gaultree scenes (IV, i, ii, iii)?
3. Do you think it is true that *2 Henry IV* is always making its audience feel guilty about one or another of its responses?
4. List as many as you can of the various ways that *2 Henry IV* echoes *1 Henry IV*.
5. Consider the extent to which the televised performance of *2 Henry IV* is an essay on the play by the director. What did he say by his choices of actors and settings? Did the production emphasize elements not emphasized in the text? Did the production "soft-pedal" any elements? Did the production do anything to make the play or elements in it less disturbing than they might otherwise have been? What was cut and to what effect?

ANSWER KEY

Answers to Multiple-choice Question
1. a, b, d, f (evidence throughout the play)
2. c (Induction [prologue] and I, i)
3. c (IV, ii)
4. b (IV, v)
5. c (V, v)
6. e (IV, v)
7. b (II, ii)
8. e (II, i; V, v; I, ii)
9. c (IV, v)
10. b (V, v)

Suggested Answers to Short-answer Essay Questions
1. (a) The Page, who serves as foil for Falstaff's first comic speeches (I, ii), thereafter appears regularly throughout the play (II, i, ii, and iv; III, ii [the Quarto text specifies him as the attendant who enters with Bardolph at line 51]; V, i, iii, and v), but he says little and does nothing of consequence. Shakespeare may have so systematically kept us mindful of Falstaff's little Page to ensure the full rhetorical effect of his casual inclusion in the company carried to prison with Falstaff when the Lord Chief Justice says "Take all his company along with him" (V, v, 93). The Page is innocent of crime or criminal intent (innocent even of the smug fatuousness that makes Shallow's embarrassing trip to jail feel just). Moreover, the Page is of Falstaff's company only because Prince Hal made him so (I, ii, 10–14; II, ii, 65–67). When the audience sees the Page casually swept up in the aftermath of the new Hal's responsible, kingly decree, it is made just that more aware of the private injustice that attends on the just action that Hal takes for the public good.

(b) In Davy's two scenes Shakespeare goes to some pains to establish him as a servant more dutiful and responsible about his master's business and welfare than his master is (V, i, 7–22; V, iii, 7–16). We are thus invited to admire young Davy for traits of the sort young Hal lacks, needs to acquire, and finally does acquire. On the other hand, Shakespeare also shows us Davy's casually cynical, Falstaff-like misuse of his association with a man of authority to pervert justice for friendship's sake (V, i, 33–46). Davy thus embodies simplified manifestations both of the principal virtue and of the principal vice that clash so uncomfortably at the end of the play.

(c) The three grooms who begin the last scene cause it immediately to echo II, iv, the big tavern scene—a scene that also begins with three servants who, like the groom, await Prince Hal's arrival in an altered guise in which he will surprise Falstaff.

2. The scene gives an audience some sense that time passes between Falstaff's departure from Gloucestershire at the end of V, iii and his arrival in London to see the coronation procession in V, v. More important, however, the arrest of Doll (with Quickly included as if for incidental good measure) provides the audience with a model by which to forecast the fate of Falstaff and the rest of his associates and the miscarriage of their false hopes. Note that the scene not only concerns associates of Falstaff but is otherwise made up of elements that suggest him and concerns that relate to him. The chief visual feature of the scene is Doll, stuffed out with pillows to look pregnant; and a good third of the scene is spent on the topic of the Beadle's extreme thinness. (Note that the comic confusion in Quickly's despondent "O God, that right should thus overcome might!" comes ironically close to stating the intellectual confusion of an audience appalled when mighty right so easily overcomes not only what might have been for Falstaff but the might of Falstaff's hold on our affections.)

3. Rumor, "painted full of tongues" and concerned with the power of hollow words, is echoed in Pistol, who is all talk and who at the end of the play brings Falstaff the accurate news that Hal is now king and the inaccurate news that Falstaff is "now one of the greatest men in this realm" (V, iii, 86). (Note the lines about winds and news with which Falstaff and Pistol greet each other in V, iii [83–95]; they echo the language of the first half of Rumor's speech.) The actor who played Northumberland—old, ineffectual, confused, and isolated—could have underscored the likeness between Northumberland (who is last seen in II, iii) and old, ineffectual, confused, isolated Shallow (who first appears in II, ii), or old, ineffectual, confused, isolated Henry IV (who first appears in III, i), by playing one or the other of those parts. Poins vanishes early in both Henry IV plays (after II, iv of *2 Henry IV*), and Prince John arrives late in both plays (in IV, ii of *2 Henry IV*). Each is a young man specifically and regularly compared to Hal. Each is disadvantaged by being a younger son. They are also alike in thinking up tricks: Poins conceives the comic disguise plots against Falstaff at Gad's Hill in *1 Henry IV* and at the tavern in *2 Henry IV*; Prince John's trick at Gaultree is similarly clever and dissimilarly serious in its intent and consequences.

4. Shakespeare makes a point of presenting Prince John's prediction—a prediction his historically informed audience knows to be accurate—as mere guesswork and the product of rumor: "I will lay odds . . ."; "I heard a bird so sing" (V, v, 106, 108). The Epilogue turned out to have been itself a rumor, part true and part false: Shakespeare did continue the story and did make us merry with fair Katherine of France, but Falstaff does not appear in *Henry V*.

THE LIFE OF KING HENRY THE FIFTH

INTRODUCTION TO THE PLAY

The Life of King Henry the Fifth is the final episode in the historical tetralogy known as the "Henriad," which begins with *Richard II* and includes both parts of *Henry IV*. The action of *Henry V* centers on the young king's reign from 1414, two years after his accession to the throne, to his betrothal to Katherine, daughter of King Charles VI of France. The highlight of this period of his reign, and of the play, is Henry's victory at Agincourt, ensuring the success of the English claim to the French throne and its land.

In *Henry V,* the new king's character has emerged. Unlike the Prince Hal of *1 and 2 Henry IV,* his character as an exemplary king is now set and remains fairly constant throughout the play. You will recall that his beginnings were, at best, inauspicious. He was mentioned only in passing in *Richard II* as Bolingbroke's "unthrifty son" who caroused in London taverns with dissolute companions, occasionally robbing local citizens. The two parts of *Henry IV* dealt largely with Hal's unprincipled escapades with the jocund reprobate, Sir John Falstaff, and his madcap companions—the first play concluding with Hal's conversion to responsible prince at the battle of Shrewsbury, and the second ending with the Prince's deathbed reconciliation with his father, and succession to his throne. Now he is an almost-ideal monarch: virtuous, heroic, inspiring, warm, gifted with a sense of humor, decisive, firm, and touched with compassion for his subjects. Toward his enemies, Henry is at first ruthless as an opponent and then forgiving as a conqueror. There is no sign in Henry V of the indolent wastrel of his youth.

This measure of discontinuity between the former Prince Hal and the present Henry V is echoed in the reduced "carry over" of characters from *2 Henry IV*. Whereas a dozen personalities were continued from *1 Henry IV* into its sequel, this number is reduced to seven in *Henry V*. There are the four historical personages of the English court—Henry, the Earl of Westmoreland, the Earl of Warwick, and the Duke of Gloucester—but of the tavern "world" of the Henriad, only three remain—Bardolph, Pistol, and Mistress Quickly—and their roles are vastly reduced. Even the great Falstaff never appears in this play, dying *in absentia*. References to earlier events and other personalities in the tetralogy are also much reduced. This play can, in great measure, though not completely, stand and be understood by itself.

In *Henry V,* it is the nobility and constancy of the character of Henry himself that serves as the chief element of unity, rather than the plot, which many critics feel is not particularly well constructed. There are too many clusters of people and too many distracting subplots; consequently, the action appears to proceed in a jumpy and disjointed fashion, with many of the transitions being abrupt and awkward. Towering above all else, however, is the figure of Henry. He almost overwhelms all the other components of the play.

As you read the text of *Henry V,* there are a number of items you should observe and keep in mind as the play progresses. First, notice the distinct clusters of characters. There are five: the members of the English court, the members of the French court and nobility, the officers of the English army, the common soldiers of the English army, and the remnant members of the "tavern realm" so boisterously depicted in the two preceding plays. Each cluster of characters engages in its own series of activities during the course of the play, and the members of each seldom interact with the members of any other cluster. Only Henry V moves freely among them; nevertheless, he remains clearly a member of only the English court. Notice, too, the development or disintegration of a number of these clusters. For example, the contingent of English nobles that Henry leads solidifies as the play progresses; while the tavern habitués, a group of which Henry was once a member and a group now leaderless following Falstaff's death, fall apart. Similarly, the initial unity and strength of the French nobility deteriorate during the preparations for the battle at Agincourt and stabilize only in defeat with the gracious amnesty and friendship offered by Henry as a result of his betrothal to Katherine.

Notice that while Shakespeare allows the character of Henry to dominate the play, he also elects not to excise certain historical events that reflect poorly on the hero. For example, Shakespeare makes it appear that the three conspirators against the king—Lord Scroop, Sir Thomas Grey, and the Earl of Cambridge—were executed without trial. Shakespeare allows Henry's complex justification of his claim to the French throne to be less than watertight. After fighting to maintain this claim, Henry V fails to ascend to the French throne. Shakespeare chooses also to include Henry's controversial mass execution of the French prisoners—an aspect of Henry's reign that is much to his historical discredit—and then provides a number of somewhat contradictory rationales for this decision. Shakespeare's Henry V may be a bit bigger than life, but he is allowed to have his faults as well.

In his essay, "Seeing *Henry V* 'Perspectively,' " Philip McGuire challenges the assumption that the "disjointed" plot is a weakness or limitation of the play. He likens the in-focus and then out-of-focus quality of the many themes and subplots of the play to perspective paintings and drawings of the

Renaissance. He places *Henry V* not only into the perspective of the Henriad but also of the tetralogy that deals with ensuing events—*1, 2, and 3 Henry VI* and *Richard III*. McGuire's perspective observations include Henry's direct relationships to the members of the several clusters of characters that populate the play, as well as the more indirect relationships these clusters have with one another. He illustrates how events, conversations, images, and even entire themes are echoed, paralleled, and counterbalanced throughout the play, suggesting that the criticism of the plot in *Henry V* is not justified and that, viewed from a certain perspective, Shakespeare did indeed construct a well-knit play.

LESSON ASSIGNMENTS

In order to get the most out of the specially designed introductory material and to appreciate the unique qualities of the play itself, Philip McGuire strongly recommends that you prepare yourself in the following manner:
- Read the synopsis of *Henry V* in this guide.
- Read the text of *Henry V*.
- Read "Seeing *Henry V* 'Perspectively' " by Philip McGuire in this guide.
- Reread the text of *Henry V*.
- View the television production.
- Complete the Self-test at the end of this lesson.

LEARNING OBJECTIVES

After completing the reading assignments and viewing the televised drama production, you should be able to:
1. Give examples of how Shakespeare omits or alters historical "facts" in *Henry V*.
2. Demonstrate how Shakespeare organizes *Henry V* so that scenes "comment upon" one another.
3. List the various opinions of Henry held by different characters and compare them to the opinions you have formed after reading the text and after watching the television production.
4. Describe the functions of the Chorus.
5. Identify the different groups of characters who make up the English army as Shakespeare presents it and describe the attitudes and concerns distinctive to each group.
6. Compare and contrast the French and English courts and armies as they appear in *Henry V*.
7. Describe the blend of epic and comic elements in *Henry V*.
8. Summarize Henry's conception of the relationship between a king and his subjects.
9. Cite moments in *Henry V* that are enriched by an awareness of the other plays in Shakespeare's "second" tetralogy.

SYNOPSIS OF THE PLAY
ACT I

The Chorus asks the audience's cooperation in imagining onstage the two monarchies (England and France), the kings, armies, and horses that are to serve as the setting for this play.

The ARCHBISHOP OF CANTERBURY and the BISHOP OF ELY are worried about a bill before the King that would confiscate all the Church's secular property. They are pleased by the King's recent metamorphosis from wastrel to statesman; as an alternative to the bill, Canterbury has offered the King a large sum of money. He has also suggested that the King press his claim to the French throne inherited from Edward III, his great-grandfather.

HENRY V asks and receives Canterbury's assurances of the justice of his claim and of the inapplicability of the obscure Salic law the French have invoked. The prelate cites scriptural authority supporting Henry's claim and is supported by the other noblemen present (the DUKE OF EXETER and the EARL OF WESTMORELAND).

Henry receives the FRENCH AMBASSADOR, who is accompanied by servants carrying a barrel of tennis balls and who delivers an insulting message from the DAUPHIN OF FRANCE rejecting the English claim and suggesting that the frivolous youth stick to tennis. Henry replies he will play a match all France will regret and then orders immediate preparations for the invasion of France.

ACT II

The Chorus describes these preparations and informs the audience of a French-financed conspiracy to assassinate Henry V, involving the EARL OF CAMBRIDGE, LORD SCROOP, and SIR EDMUND GREY.

BARDOLPH, a lieutenant, and NYM, a corporal, meet PISTOL, an *auncient* (ensign), and his new wife MISTRESS QUICKLY. Swords drawn, Nym and Pistol spar verbally over money. FALSTAFF's servant, BOY, calls Quickly to his sick master's bedside. Quickly returns to announce Sir John is dying. The quarrel ends, and all leave to visit their friend.

In the presence of the Dukes of Exeter and BEDFORD and the EARL OF WESTMORELAND, Henry first extracts assurances of loyalty from each conspirator. He then frees a man arrested earlier for treasonous speech and, when the three conspirators protest this leniency, Henry confronts them with their own treason and condemns each to the death they had just advocated for other traitors.

112   The Life of King Henry the Fifth

On their way to join the English invasion forces assembling at Southampton, Bardolph, Nym, and Pistol, together with Boy and Quickly, discuss the details of Falstaff's death.

Before the assembled nobility in the French court, KING CHARLES reviews the political and military situation and orders the inspection and repair of the defenses. An overconfident Dauphin and the cautious CONSTABLE disagree on the strength of the English and the outlook for France. As Henry's ambassador, Exeter demands the surrender of the French crown. The King demurs but the Dauphin remains defiant.

ACT III

The Chorus asks the audience to imagine a vulnerable England stripped of its young men, the great English fleet crossing the Channel to Harfleur, and the siege of that city. The French king has offered his daughter, KATHERINE, and some unprofitable dukedoms to persuade Henry to cancel the invasion. Henry has refused.

In an eloquent harrangue invoking pride in English values and ancestry, Henry exhorts his troops to greater effort; however, in the very next scene, we see the opposite: Bardolph, Nym, and Pistol make a show of fighting but hang back instead. Boy remarks on their cowardice and immorality and vows to leave their service. The Welsh Captains FLUELLEN and GOWER discuss the siege and criticize the mining operations under the command of Captain MACMORRIS, an Irishman, who later joins the discussion along with Captain JAMY, a Scot. Fluellen and Macmorris punctuate their argument with ethnic jibes, but when swords are drawn, Gower intervenes.

At the walls of Harfleur, Henry warns of the mayhem the English troops will wreak should the city continue to resist. The GOVERNOR capitulates, and he is replaced by Exeter who is charged by Henry to be merciful.

Far removed from the battle, Katherine earnestly tries to learn English from her attendant, ALICE, in a scene conducted entirely in French and broken English. At the French Court, the Constable and the Dauphin offer divided counsel: the former, ashamed of the French performance, urging the immediate engagement of the sick and exhausted English armies, the latter, insufferably overconfident, remaining contemptuous of the English threat. Charles orders all noblemen to the front except the Dauphin who, insubordinate, almost refuses.

En route to Calais, the English fight to hold the only remaining bridge across the Somme River. Returning from the battle, Fluellen praises the gallantry of Exeter and Pistol. Pistol asks Fluellen to intercede with Exeter to save Bardolph from execution for having looted a church of a religious artifact. Fluellen refuses, for discipline must be enforced, and is reviled by

Pistol. Gower then informs Fluellen of Pistol's true character. Henry upholds the sentence and repeats his order that the French people not be coerced in any way.

MONTJOY, a French herald, delivers a demand that Henry pay a ransom and compensate France for its losses. Henry refuses. Admitting his army is weak and sickly, he requests clear passage to Calais but vows to fight if challenged.

In the predawn darkness of the French camp, French noblemen, including the Dauphin, the Constable, and DUKE OF ORLEANS, engage in frivolous boasting about their horses. When a messenger reports the approach of the English, the noblemen contemptuously assess the English chances of victory.

ACT IV

The Chorus describes the two opposing camps, contrasting the confident French playing dice with the worn-out and pensive English huddled about their campfires.

Henry confides his worries to his brother, the DUKE OF GLOUCESTER. Then, disguised in a cloak borrowed from SIR THOMAS ERPINGHAM, he moves about the camp. He meets Pistol who, believing "HARRY LE ROI" to be just another Welshman, asks him to deliver a challenge to Fluellen. Later, Henry encounters three soldiers—BATES, COURT, and WILLIAMS—and the four debate whether the King should be told of the desperate plight of the troops, whether he should pay the ransom, the justness of the King's cause, and whether the King is responsible for the sins of soldiers killed in battle. Still disguised, Henry replies that subjects owe allegiance to the King, who is not responsible for the condition of their souls. When Williams challenges Henry's defense of the King's trustworthiness, the two agree to a duel after the impending battle. After they leave, Henry delivers a plaintive soliloquy on the burdens of kingship, expressing envy for the slave who sleeps soundly. He is then called into council.

The French noblemen again engage in lighthearted, prebattle banter and this time are joined by the usually reserved Constable. In the English camp, Henry delivers a confident exhortation to an anxious Westmoreland, predicting that Englishmen who fight at Agincourt will win a glorious niche in English history. After declining a last French offer for ransom, Henry accords the DUKE OF YORK the honor of leading the forward line.

In a comic scene, Pistol, with Boy serving as mastermind and interpreter, not only deceives and captures a French nobleman but gets a ransom as well. Both Bardolph and Nym are reported as hanged, and Boy, in revealing the vulnerability of the English camp, augurs his own fate. In another battlefield scene, the Constable and other French leaders admit they are beaten but continue to fight. Back in the English lines, Exeter describes the death of York and Suffolk and delivers York's dying message to Henry. Hearing of French reinforcements, Henry orders the slaughter of all prisoners. Fluellen and Gower then indignantly discuss the French encirclement of the English camp and the slaughter of the defenseless wounded and noncombatant servants, and Fluellen enthusiastically compares Henry to Alexander the Great. Hearing of the French deed, Henry (again) orders the execution of French prisoners. Montjoy arrives to admit defeat and request permission to gather the dead.

Williams arrives with Henry's glove in his cap looking for its counterpart in another cap to consummate the challenge. Henry induces Fluellen to wear William's glove in his cap as a practical joke, but asks Gloucester and the EARL OF WARWICK to see no harm comes to either party. When the joke is revealed, Williams is not amused but accepts a monetary settlement from the King. More soberly, Henry receives the casualty report and ascribes the victory to God.

ACT V

In broad strides, the Chorus leaps over time and geography to report Henry's triumphant return to England, the failure of the Holy Roman Emperor to negotiate a peace, and Henry's return to France.

Fluellen, with a leek in his cap, searches out Pistol to consummate their separate challenge. Fluellen beats Pistol until the latter has completely swallowed the malodorous herb and is thoroughly humiliated. When Pistol tries to boast after Fluellen has left, Gower excoriates the rogue.

At Troyes, Henry listens to a speech of praise by the DUKE OF BURGUNDY in the presence of the French king and queen, and then appoints a commission of five English lords to meet with the King and Burgundy to settle the articles of peace. Then follows one of the great romantic scenes of Shakespeare, during which Henry bluntly woos, proposes, and wins over Katherine. When the negotiators return, Henry demands and receives Kate as his wife, along with all his other demands, though he will remain only as heir to France until Charles's death. The Eiplogue reports that the French throne was left to Henry's son, Henry VI, whose mismanaged reign resulted in the loss of France.

Seeing *Henry V* "Perspectively"

Philip C. McGuire

The more intently one eyes it, the more perplexing *The Life of King Henry the Fifth* becomes. The Prologue proclaims that we will watch an English epic devoted to the heroic deeds of "warlike Harry," but the play opens with two bishops agreeing that the best way to protect church property is to have Henry wage war against the French. Shakespeare concludes the play just as oddly—not with the remarkable victory of Henry's tiny army at Agincourt but with one minor character humiliating another and with the peace negotiations between France and England, which then move offstage while Henry woos Katherine. The only actual combat during the battle of Agincourt that Shakespeare explicitly requires to be enacted onstage is also a bit unexpected. We see a cowardly Frenchman surrender to an Englishman whose own cowardice has been well established. Just as strangely, one of the most memorable passages in the play is a moving account of the final moments of a character, Falstaff, who never appears onstage. In addition, at the beginning of each act, a remarkably talkative Chorus insists on telling us much more than the background information we need to make sense of what follows. Often, what does follow—for example, the quarrel between Nym and Pistol, or between Fluellen and Macmorris, Katherine's English lesson, the Dauphin's praise of his horse—seems to have little bearing on the announced subject of *Henry V:* the epic achievements of the heroic Harry.

In the words Burgundy speaks to Henry near the end of *Henry V,* Shakespeare seems to advise us on how best to look at this oddly perplexing play. After wooing Katherine, Henry declares that love has made him blind; he says he "cannot see many a fair French city for one fair French maid that stands in my way" (V, ii, 304–6). Burgundy responds, "Yes, my lord, you see them perspectively, the cities turned into a maid; for they are all girdled with maiden walls that war hath never entered" (V, ii, 307–10). Watching and reading *Henry V* we must see "perspectively"—cultivating the capacity to see as one things as disparate as maidens and cities, persons as antithetical as Pistol and the Dauphin, and events as dissimilar as the report of Falstaff's death and Katherine's English lesson. Like a Renaissance perspective glass, *Henry V* generates multiple images of the historical persons and events it treats by refracting them through the lenses of other people and other events.

We should also see *Henry V* as a work that, like the perspective paintings and drawings of the Renaissance, is put together in such a way that various details and moments come into and move out of focus as the play's structure—its arrangement of events—compels its audience to assume new angles of vision, new perspectives. The opening scene of Act III offers a clear example of this process. Our initial sense of the force of Henry's stirring call "Once more unto the breach, dear friends, once more" (III, i, 1) is altered when, immediately after Henry and those with him charge on the cry of " 'God for Harry! England and Saint George!' " (III, i, 34), Bardolph and his companions enter. Bardolph urges others to press forward in words echoing the King's— "On, on, on, on, on! to the breach, to the breach!" (III, ii, 1)—but he and his companions remain motionless. They refuse to advance to that place where "knocks go and come; God's vassals drop and die" (III, ii, 6) until Fluellen drives them forward with blows and with words far less eloquent than Henry's or even Bardolph's: "Up to the preach, you dogs!" (III, ii, 18). Later in that same scene, the courage Henry displays and, by example as well as eloquence, inspires in (most of) his soldiers is put into still another perspective. As we hear Fluellen and the other captains discuss using mines to destroy the walls of Harfleur, we realize that the gallant charge we saw earlier has proved more valiant than effective. When Harfleur does eventually yield, it is not because English courage has smashed its defenses and not because Henry's merciless threat to kill all inhabitants has cowed the defenders, but because the Dauphin's "powers are not yet ready/To raise so great a siege" (III, iii, 46–47). Through such shifting perspectives the play establishes with striking force Henry's qualities of courage, eloquence, and leadership and then proceeds to demonstrate the limits of their effectiveness.

We must also see *Henry V* "perspectively" in other ways. The Epilogue requires that our response to the play be informed by some knowledge of what ensued after Henry's death:

> *Henry the Sixth, in infant bands crowned King*
>   *Of France and England, did this king succeed;*
> *Whose state so many had the managing*
>   *That they lost France and made his England bleed.*
>
>   (Epi., 9–12)

By reminding us of the subsequent loss of all that Henry gained while "fortune made his sword" (Epi., 6)—a subject treated in Shakespeare's "first"[1] tetralogy composed of *1, 2, and 3 Henry VI* and *Richard III*—the Epilogue insists that our admiration of Henry's accomplishments include an awareness of their transience: "Small time; but in that small most greatly lived/This Star of England" (Epi., 5–6).

While complete in and of itself, *Henry V* is also the final, completing element of a larger artistic whole, Shakespeare's "second" tetralogy, which, commencing with *Richard II* and embracing *1 and 2 Henry IV,* deals with the years preceding Henry V's reign. Seen in terms of those plays and of that tetralogy, characters, events, and patterns in *Henry V* take on added richness and deeper unity. For example, Henry's concern with the potential threat posed by the Scots if he invades France bespeaks a prudence that contrasts favorably with the impulsiveness that prompted Richard II to lead an expedition against the Irish,[2] a decision that allowed Bolingbroke (Henry's father and later Henry IV) to land his army in England without challenge.

Consider, as another example, how awareness of the moment in *2 Henry IV* when the newly crowned Henry V rejects Falstaff puts several moments in *Henry V* in new perspectives:

> FALSTAFF: *My king! My Jove!*[3] *I speak to thee, my heart!*
> KING: *I know thee not, old man. Fall to thy prayers.*
> . . . .
> *Presume not that I am the think I was,*
> *For God doth know, so shall the world perceive,*
> *That I have turned away my former self.*
> *So will I those that kept me company.*
> *When thou dost hear I am as I have been,*
> *Approach me, and thou shalt be as thou wast,*
> *The tutor and the feeder of my riots.*
> *Till then, I banish thee, on pain of death,*
> *As I have done the rest of my misleaders,*
> *Not to come near our person by ten mile.*
>
> (V, v, 47–66)

Many of the scenes in *Henry V* that seem least related to Henry's heroic deeds are peopled by "the rest of my misleaders": Nym, Bardolph, Pistol, Hostess Quickly, and Boy. Shakespeare conveys Henry's effectiveness in turning them away by a simple theatrical device: Only once in *Henry V* do we see Henry in the presence of even one of "those that kept me company." On that single occasion, Henry, having declared that he does not "know" Falstaff, proceeds to *act* as if he does not know Pistol when, disguised, he meets him on the eve of Agincourt. Pistol, for his part, *seems*[4] not to know to whom he is speaking when he expresses his love for King Henry in terms that, initially at least, more accurately describe the prank-prone young man he knew as Prince Hal:

> *The king's a bawcock, and a heart of gold,*
> *A lad of life, an imp of fame,*
> *Of parents good, of first most valiant.*
> *I kiss his dirty shoe, and from heartstring*
> *I love the lovely bully.*
>
> (IV, i, 44–48)

When Fluellen reports on a skirmish with the French, he advises Henry that the only English casualty is "one that is like to be executed for robbing a church—one Pardolph, if your majesty know the man" (III, vi, 97–99), and he proceeds to give a detailed description of Bardolph's distinctive physiognomy. Henry's response seems untempered by the fact that Bardolph is one of those with whom he once caroused: "We would have all such offenders so cut off" (III, vi, 103). The need for discipline within the army demands that Henry not know Bardolph, just as the obligations of kingship demanded that he tell Falstaff "I know thee not, old man."

One can argue that Henry *must* turn away and not know such men as Falstaff, Bardolph, and Pistol if he is to achieve his full stature as heroic king and commander. Fluellen, who invokes "the disciplines of the war" (III, ii, 54) as the norm for all conduct, regards Henry's treatment of Falstaff as proof that his king is superior to one of the most famous of all conquerors, Alexander the Great. Fluellen explains to Gower,

> *As Alexander killed his friend Cleitus, being in his ales and cups, so also Harry Monmouth, being in his right wits and his good judgments, turned away the fat knight with the great pelly doublet.*

(IV, vii, 40–44)

Gower may be right when he says of Henry, "He never killed any of his friends" (IV, vii, 36–37), but his words must be balanced against Hostess Quickly's remark when she learns that Falstaff is dying: "The king has killed his heart" (II, i, 84).[5] What Bardolph's hanging and Falstaff's death make clear—painfully so if they are emphasized in performance[6]—is that the king who triumphs so miraculously at Agincourt is a man who is willing to stand by passively or be absent as those who *were* his friends go to their deaths.

Hostess Quickly's heartfelt if jumbled description of Falstaff's death allows us to know that, as if in accordance with Henry's command "Fall to thy prayers," he dies at prayer—not babbling "of green fields" but reciting the Twenty-third Psalm[7] and crying out, " 'God, God, God!' three or four times" (II, iii, 16–19). Quickly's account of how she touched different parts of Falstaff's dying body parallels the scene in which Princess Katherine learns the English names for parts of the body as she touches them. As Quickly's hands move "upward and upward" from Falstaff's feet toward his genitals, she finds that "all was as cold as any stone" (II, iii, 24); similarly, Katherine's lesson brings her to the word *foot* which, as she (mis)pronounces it, sounds like the French word *foutre,* a vulgarism meaning "to copulate." The shifting between English and French during Katherine's lesson leads to that sexual pun, and viewed "perspectively," that movement enacts, in miniature as it were, the process whereby the deadly differences between French and English (the peoples as well as the languages) are reconciled by the betrothal and imminent sexual union of Katherine and Henry.

In moving toward and concluding with a betrothal, *Henry V* conforms to a pattern typical of a comedy and evident in such Shakespearean plays as *Twelfth Night* and *As You Like It.* In effect, Shakespeare, in this play, crosses a comic pattern with material—battles, deaths, heroism—appropriate for an epic. The scenes in which the rest of Henry's "misleaders" appear are among the funniest in the play, yet they establish a pattern that is anticomic. In them the movement is not toward sexual unity and the establishment of a society more inclusive and less flawed than what preceded it. Instead, we see a process of fragmentation and dissolution. While it is a marriage that reconciles the English and the French, it is a marriage newly made (between Pistol and Hostess Quickly) that sets Nym and Pistol, cowards both, to quarreling with swords drawn. By the end of that scene, the first of several in which we see men who are ostensibly comrades nearly come to blows, Pistol and Nym are reconciled—with Bardolph's help—once Pistol agrees to pay *part* of the gambling debt he owes to Nym:

A noble shalt thou have, and present pay;
And liquor likewise will I give to thee,
And friendship shall combine, and brotherhood.
I'll live by Nym, and Nym shall live by me.

(II, i, 103–6)

During the play we watch Henry's multinational army of quarrelsome troops become "friends" and then an even more tightly knit unit whom Henry calls, despite their differences in rank and social class,

We few, we happy few, we band of brothers;
For he to-day that sheds his blood with me
Shall be my brother.

(IV, iii, 60–62)

However, as we watch Henry's army coalesce into a "fellowship" (IV, iii, 39), we also see another smaller group who are combined in "friendship" and "brotherhood" come apart. The dismembering of the fellowship of Nym, Bardolph, Pistol, and Boy begins when Boy, realizing that his companions "will steal anything, and call it purchase," resolves to "leave them and seek some better service" (III, ii, 38, 47). Bardolph is hanged for stealing and Nym suffers the same fate, we learn from Boy, just before he himself is killed when the French attack the defenseless boys in the English camp. Of that small band who set off for France, only Pistol survives—humiliated but alive—to return, alone, to an England where nobody waits for him:

News have I, that my Doll is dead i' th' spital
Of a malady of France;
And there my rendezvous is quite cut off.

(V, i, 73–75)

Quickly's death, of a venereal disease, suggests how sexual activity can endanger rather than engender life, and it marks the end of a marriage whose beginning we saw earlier in the play. Shakespeare chooses a crucial point to make us aware of how that marriage concludes: immediately before we watch arrangements made for a marriage that will combine—it is hoped—the hearts, the bodies, and the realms of Katherine and Henry in lasting union. To signify their impending marriage, Katherine and Henry exchange kisses—first in private, then in public—and those kisses, marking a moment of coming together, contrast tellingly with the kisses that Quickly, whom we never see again, gave to her new husband Pistol and the rest of Prince Hal's "misleaders" (except Nym) when, following Falstaff's death, they set off for France.

In addition to being anticomical in their cumulative impact, the scenes involving Henry's former "misleaders" also moderate the play's emphasis on the heroic. A good deal of that emphasis arises from the Chorus. It describes those who go with Henry to France as "culled and choice-drawn cavaliers" (III, Cho., 24), and it exalts their motives: "honor's thought/Reigns solely in the breasts of every man" (II, Cho., 3–4). Henry's army, however, includes the likes of Pistol, Bardolph, and Nym, and their motives, Pistol makes clear, are more mercenary and parasitical than honorable: "Yoke-fellows in arms,/ Let us to France, like horseleeches, my boys,/To suck, to suck, the very blood to suck!" (II, iii, 49–51). Before the walls of Harfleur, Bardolph calls for *others* to follow Harry into the breach the cannon has blown, Nym admits that "the knocks are too hot; and, for mine own part, I have not a case of lives," and Boy prefers "an alehouse in London" to what the battlefield offers: "I would give all my fame for a pot of ale and safety" (III, ii, 2–3, 10–11). As a group and as individuals, they prefer life-preserving cowardice to heroism, and their blunt emphasis on profiting from and surviving the war by any means necessary plays against the values that the nobles, French as well as English, invoke as they go to battle.

For the noblemen, war is an opportunity to win not so much victory as fame, to garner glory rather than profit. The nobility repeatedly speak of war as a form of agonistic play, a kind of competitive sport. On the eve of Agincourt, the French nobility compete by comparing their armor and horses, in anticipation of the competition in displaying valor and taking Englishmen they will engage in when morning comes. Even as he urges his men "once more into the breach," Henry employs a metaphor which, mixing elements of racing and hunting, reveals the connection between sport and battle typical of the nobility's conception of war: "I see you stand like greyhounds in the slips,/Straining upon the start. The game's afoot!" (III, i, 31–32). The same conception surfaces as Henry justifies Bardolph's execution: "when lenity and cruelty play for a kingdom, the gentler gamester is the soonest winner" (III, vi, 107–9). The Dauphin's mocking gift of tennis balls stirs Henry to compare the war he is about to begin to a tennis match:

> *When we have matched our rackets to these balls,*
> *We will in France, by God's grace, play a set*
> *Shall strike his father's crown into the hazard.*

(I, ii, 262–64)

For Henry, the war is, in part at least, a matter of personal honor, and he proceeds to turn the Dauphin's mock back upon him just as Fluellen turns Pistol's mock upon him by forcing him to eat a leek. In each instance, one person vindicates his honor and courage by demonstrating another's lack of those qualities. By the play's end both the Dauphin and Pistol stand exposed as braggart soldiers—men whose deeds fall far short of their boasts.

Shakespeare provides a third perspective upon war by means of Fluellen the Welshman and his fellow captains: Gower the Englishman, Macmorris the Irishman, and Jamy the Scotsman. Despite explosive differences in the national temperaments of which each is a caricature, they share the view that war is neither a sporting activity provided to enhance one's honor nor an unparalleled opportunity to steal. For them war is a vocation, a profession to be studied and then practiced in accordance with certain rules and principles— what Fluellen calls "the disciplines of the war." According to those "disciplines," Bardolph must hang for stealing, and the French slaughter of the boys in the English camp is a heinous deed—" 'Tis expressly against the law of arms" (IV, vii, 1-2)—that justifies, in Gower's mind, the King's order to kill all prisoners. However, for all their concern with the right and wrong ways of fighting a war, the captains, in their professionalism, never ponder the issue of the morality of the war itself.

That issue arises, however, in the conversation between Henry in disguise and Bates, Williams, and Court. Those three privates look upon war not as a profession nor as an opportunity to gain either glory or goods but as a duty imposed on them as subjects by their King. The question of whether, in going to war, the King's cause is "just and his quarrel honorable" is, William says, "more than we know" (IV, i, 122-23). Bates adds,

> *Ay, or more than we should seek after, for we know enough if we know we are the king's subjects. If his cause be wrong, our obedience to the king wipes the crime of it out of us.*
>
> (IV, i, 124-27)

In such a case, Williams points out, the crime is the king's:

> *But if the cause be not good, the king himself hath a heavy reckoning to make when all those legs and arms and heads, chopped off in a battle, shall join together at the latter day and cry all, "We died at such a place"*
>
> (IV, i, 127-31)

Henry denies the King's responsibility for the souls of those who die in battle and reasons that war is itself an instrument of morality. God uses it to punish evildoers who have eluded human justice, and it provides each man with an opportunity to prepare for death by examining the state of his soul:

> *Therefore should every soldier in the wars do as every sick man in his bed—wash every mote out of his conscience; and dying so, death is to him*

> *advantage; or not dying, the time was blessedly lost wherein such preparation was gained....*
>
> (IV, i, 168–72)

Some will agree with Henry—as Bates and Williams do—that "the king is not to answer it" if his soldiers die spiritually "ill" (IV, i, 176–77). Henry's definition of the individual man's public obligations and his private responsibilities remains eloquently compelling for many: "Every subject's duty is the king's, but every subject's soul is his own" (IV, i, 166–68).

Others, however, might withhold assent, perhaps because throughout his conversation with the dutiful privates Henry takes for granted—as we cannot—that his cause is just and his quarrel honorable. Shakespeare's opening scene poses the question of the legitimacy of Henry's claim to the throne of France in a way that makes it difficult for us to agree, with Bates, that the answer is "more than we should seek after." Our knowledge that self-interest prompts the bishops' assurances that Henry's claim is valid—coupled with what might strike many as the obscurity of Canterbury's exposition of the Salic law—means that we are denied the certainty, at times verging on self-righteousness, that Shakespeare gives to Henry. To say that we cannot share Henry's conviction that his cause is just is not, however, to say that we are therefore certain that it is *not* just. Shakespeare raises the issue of the validity of Henry's claim without giving us, in the play, the means to resolve it. In effect, *Henry V* prompts us to "seek after" an answer, a certainty, that is established as being—in Williams' words—"more than we know."

By denying us ground for a certainty equivalent to Henry's, Shakespeare leads us on to see the war "perspectively." War, as Shakespeare presents it in *Henry V,* is a phenomenon that both fits and eludes the categories brought to bear upon it. It is, simultaneously and variously, a noble contest, an occasion for pillage, an exercise of professional skill, a moral duty, a tool of divine justice, and a spur to moral self-scrutiny. It inspires heroism as well as cowardice and even love in those caught up in it. Henry's army becomes a "band of brothers," united in mutual interdependence, and York dies kissing Suffolk's corpse, the two of them "espoused to death" and—in a manner befitting Romeo and Juliet—sealing with their blood "a testament of noble-ending love" (IV, vi, 26–27). But war also engenders the resolve necessary to be willing to hang a man even if "he were my brother" (III, vi, 53) or—as Bardolph was—a former companion of the King. War also generates such atrocities as the slaughter of the camp boys and the systematic killing of the French prisoners. Our indecision regarding the justice of Henry's cause helps us—if we resist the tendency to resort to a single, incompletely accurate perspective—to know war as an experience man must simplify in order to comprehend.

Shakespeare's characterization of Henry invites us, again, to see "perspectively." The characterization is rich with admirable features—physical, mental, and moral. Henry, the Chorus declares, is an exemplary monarch, "the mirror of all Christian kings" (II, Cho., 6). He has changed in an almost miraculous fashion, mortifying his youthful wildness from the instant that, with his father's death, he became King: "Yea, at that very moment," Canterbury insists,

> *Consideration like an angel came*
> *And whipped th' offending Adam out of him,*
> *Leaving his body as a paradise*
> *T' envelop and contain celestial spirits.*
>
> (I, i, 27–31)

Henry is pious: he consults the bishops, prays before battle, and attributes to God his triumph at Agincourt. He is eloquent, deftly employing, in situations as diverse as replying to the Dauphin, threatening Harfleur, or wooing Katherine, the powers of speech that Shakespeare's era regarded as the most direct expression of the rationality that distinguished man from the beasts. He is, as Charles of France is not, a vigorous king who leads his men in battle, and he displays personal courage that enables him, in contrast to the Dauphin, to perform acts that match his words. By winning a wife as well as a battle at Agincourt, Henry unites the martial and the marital in a way that seems beyond the powers of the Dauphin, who praises his horse in terms that other men use for the women they love (III, vii, 1–65). The night before Agincourt Henry acknowledges, as Richard II never could,[8] that he is both a man as his subjects are and a king. "The king," he tells Bates, "is but a man, as I am. . . . His ceremonies laid by, in his nakedness he appears but a man" (IV, i, 98–102). He sees through the ceremonies surrounding kingship while accepting his kingly responsibility to serve and be responsible for the welfare of his subjects, laboring sleeplessly on their behalf: "What watch the king keeps to maintain the peace,/Whose hours the peasant best advantages" (IV, i, 269–70).

One of the most famous examples of Renaissance perspective painting is Holbein's *The Ambassadors*.[9] Looked at directly, it contains an object that seems distorted but which, if one views the painting from an angle, becomes a skull. The equivalent of that skull in Shakespeare's portrait of Henry V is the slaying of the French prisoners. Gower says that "the king most worthily hath caused every soldier to cut his prisoner's throat" (IV,vii, 8–10), because the French have attacked the camp, killing the boys—an event that can have great impact if it is shown in performance or if we are made to realize that Boy is among the victims. Henry does indeed order the French prisoners executed when he learns of the slaughter, but in so doing he is repeating an order already given earlier and for a different reason: "The French have reinforced their scattered men./Then every soldier kill his prisoners!" (IV, vi, 36–37).[10]

Once we have focused upon the killing of the prisoners, it becomes easier to see that Shakespeare has presented many of Henry's positive features as having another, less admirable facet. Henry speaks, for example, of maintaining peace for the benefit of his subjects, but he does so on the eve of battle in a war he initiated. At times, Henry's piety shades into a tendency to equate his will and purposes with God's. Before Harfleur he uses his eloquence first to urge his men to act like beasts—"Then imitate the action of the tiger" (III, i, 6)—and then to give force to his threat to turn his soldiers loose without any restraints if the city continues to resist:

> *The gates of mercy shall be all shut up,*
> *And the fleshed soldier, rough and hard of heart,*
> *In liberty of bloody hand shall range*
> *With conscience wide as hell, mowing like grass*
> *Your fresh fair virgins and your flow'ring infants.*
>
> (III, iii, 10–14)

Henry's peacemaking has, at times, an unpleasantly mercenary tinge. To Burgundy's impassioned description of the disorder that war has inflicted upon "this best garden of the world,/Our fertile France," Henry responds,

> *If, Duke of Burgundy, you would the peace*
> *Whose want gives growth to th' imperfections*
> *Which you have cited, you must buy that peace*
>
> (V, ii, 36–37, 68–70)

His marriage to Katherine is as much a business transaction as an act of love. When he asks that Katherine remain with him while the others go off to settle details of the peace agreement, he speaks of her in terms that are less than passionately romantic: "She is our capital demand, comprised/Within the fore-rank of our articles" (V, ii, 96–99). After wooing Katherine with what seems like sincere ardor, Henry accepts the King of France's consent that she will be his wife only after imposing a condition:

> *I am content, so the maiden cities you talk of may wait on her. So the maid that stood in the way for my wish shall show me the way to my will.*
>
> (V, ii, 312–14)

Occasionally, traces of the prankfully deceiving Prince Hal—"the offending Adam"—whom Henry has supposedly cast off manifest themselves. His handling of the traitors Cambridge, Scroop, and Gray is one example. He tricks them by allowing them to believe that he trusts them still. Like a cat playing with mice, he allows them to give reasons why he should not pardon the man who has insulted him, then he gives them documents that show that

"I know your worthiness" (II, ii, 69). He responds to their call for mercy by saying: "The mercy that was quick in us but late,/By your own counsel is suppressed and killed" (II, ii, 79–80).

The prank that Henry plays upon Williams and Fluellen is more innocent and good-hearted, but parallels to that earlier, more Machiavellian trick emerge. Henry gives Williams's glove to Fluellen with the warning that any man who challenges it is "an enemy to our person" (IV, vii, 149–50). When he encounters Williams, Fluellen denounces him as being what Scroop, Cambridge, and Gray in fact were—a traitor—and his explanation to Warwick extends the parallel: "My Lord of Warwick, here is, praised be God for it, a most contagious treason come to light" (IV, viii, 19–20). After Henry enters and presents his own glove to Williams, he tells him "It was ourself thou didst abuse" (IV, viii, 45), thus linking him with the man pardoned earlier who had "railed against our person" (II, ii, 41). The actual traitors who had argued against pardoning that man were corrupted by golden coins—crowns—and Henry offers coins of the same kind to Williams: "Here, Uncle Exeter, fill this glove with crowns,/And give it to this fellow. . . . Give him the crowns" (IV, viii, 52–55). Charged to "be friends with him" (IV, viii, 56), Fluellen follows with a peace offering of his own: "Hold, there is twelve pence for you" (IV, viii, 58–59). The money offered by Henry and Fluellen links this quarrel to those others, which also ended with money changing hands—Nym's with Pistol over Hostess Quickly, and Fluellen's with Pistol over the leek.

Seen "perspectively," those different quarrels create a pattern pertinent to the way in which Henry settles his "quarrel" with Charles over who should wear the crown of France. On resolving to invade France, Henry had declared,

> *Or there we'll sit,*
> *Ruling in large and ample empery*
> *O'er France and all her almost kingly dukedoms,*
> *Or lay these bones in an unworthy urn,*
> *Tombless, with no remembrance over them.*
>
> (I, ii, 226–30)

Before departing for France, Henry refuses, the Chorus tells us, Charles's offer of "Katherine his daughter, and with her to dowry/Some petty and unprofitable dukedoms" (III, Cho., 30–31). The play ends, however, with Henry agreeing to a peace that brings him Katherine and certain French cities, plus the right to be called heir of France—a title whose weight is diminished by the fact that we never hear it proclaimed in English. Henry settles, in fact, for considerably less than the crown of France that he claimed was his by all rights, and we never see him fulfill his vow to rule "in large and ample empery/O'er France." Has he, one is tempted to ask, been bought off? In settling his quarrel with Charles, how different is Henry from Nym, from Pistol, or from Williams, who refuses twelve pence from Fluellen but accepts crowns from Henry?[11]

To say, however, that Shakespeare condemns Henry is to simplify the play, and to say that Shakespeare sings his undiluted praise is equally simplistic. Confronting the treacherous Scroop—"the man that was his bedfellow,/Whom he hath dulled and cloyed with gracious favors"—Henry himself remarks how difficult it is to acknowledge evil in those we love: " 'Tis so strange/That, though the truth of it stands off as gross/As black and white, my eye will scarcely see it" (II, ii, 8–9, 102–4). What Shakespeare gives us in *Henry V* is a work that makes it possible to admire and even rejoice in Henry's character and achievements without becoming blindly enamored of them. We can see Henry as Henry himself is urged to see Katherine—not blindly but "perspectively."

The Chorus is the most crucial element in Shakespeare's effort to have his audience see "perspectively," and it will be the feature of the play that the television production will find most difficult to use effectively and intelligently. Like the Chorus of *Romeo and Juliet,* the Chorus of *Henry V* serves a conventional expository function, giving the audience information needed to understand ensuing events. The Chorus of *Henry V* also stresses, less conventionally, that the play before us is a history play in which facts have been manipulated in order to meet the constraints imposed by the limits of dramatic representation and to clarify the truths and patterns underlying mere facts. For example, by skipping over events after the Battle of Agincourt—"Which cannot in their huge and proper life/Be here presented" (V, Cho., 5–6)—the play directly links Henry's victory there to the treaty agreed upon in Act V. In fact, however, Henry's triumph at Agincourt in October, 1415, marked the conclusion of the first of two campaigns in France, the second of which culminated, five years later, in the Treaty of Troyes.

Repeatedly, the Chorus of *Henry V* directs our attention to what it says are deficiencies in the play that flow directly from the limitations of the theatrical medium in which Shakespeare has chosen to work. The theater—"this unworthy scaffold," "this cockpit," "this wooden O" (Pro., 10, 11, 13)—cannot present actual kings, armies, horses, ranks of cannon, or fleets under sail. As it announces such shortcomings, the Chorus calls upon us to cooperate in remedying them. It implores us to open ourselves to the language of the play—to respond to Shakespeare's eloquence much as Henry's soldiers respond to his—and to set our minds imaginatively to work:

> *Think, when we talk of horses, that you see them*
> *Printing their proud hoofs i' th' receiving earth;*
> *For 'tis your thoughts that now must deck our kings,*
> *Carry them here and there. . . .*

(Pro., 26–29).

> [and]
>
> *Play with your fancies, and in them behold*
> *Upon the hempen tackle shipboys climbing;*
>
> ....
>
> *Work, work your thoughts, and therein see a siege:*
> *Behold the ordinance on their carriages,*
> *With fatal mouths gaping on girded Harfleur.*
>
> ....
>
> *Still be kind*
> *And eke out our performance with your mind.*
>
> (III, Cho., 7–8, 25–27, 34–35)
>
> [and]
>
> *But now behold,*
> *In the quick forge and working-house of thought,*
> *How London doth pour out her citizens!*
>
> (V, Cho., 23–24)

Calling upon us to "think," "work," and "play," the Chorus establishes correspondences between our activities as an audience and those of the characters before us. As we watch a play in which a dauphin of France mocks a king of England and Pistol mocks the leek Fluellen so proudly wears, we are made aware that the play itself is a mockery of actual events: "Yet sit and see,/Minding true things by what their mock'ries be" (IV, Cho., 52–53). In defining the King's responsibility for his subjects, Williams describes the shattering violence that combat inflicts upon the human body—"all those legs and arms and heads, chopped off in a battle" (IV, i, 128–29)—and yet we are given responsibility for peopling the stage with soldiers by imaginatively dismembering the few actors we see in front of us:

> *Piece out our imperfections with your thoughts:*
> *Into a thousand parts divide one man*
> *And make imaginary puissance.*
>
> (Pro., 23–25)

When Salisbury brings word that the French "with all expedience charge on us," Henry reassures those around him: "All things are ready, if our minds be so" (IV, iii, 70–71). The Chorus works to make our minds "ready," and that consists in part in realizing that our relationship to the actors is like that of a monarch to his subjects. Like Henry, each of us in the audience is called upon to exercise mercy, humanely accepting the limitations of those who serve us:

> *But pardon, gentles all,*
> *The flat unraisèd spirits that hath dared*
> *On this unworthy scaffold to bring forth*

> *So great an object. . . .*
> *Admit me Chorus to this history*
> *Who, Prologue-like, your humble patience pray,*
> *Gently to hear, kindly to judge, our play.*
>
> (Pro., 8–11, 32–34)

The references to "gentles all" and "gently" point to yet another correspondence between what we as an audience do and what happens on the stage. During the performance of *Henry V* we who are watching it have an opportunity to become a community—analogous to Henry's embattled "band of brothers"—in which ("gentles all") distinctions of rank and class are put aside. That community comes into being through the process of sharing, not the rigors of battle, but the experience of the play.

The Chorus of *Henry V* makes explicit our role in the play. It defines *Henry V* as a work that we help to bring into being. The Chorus insists that the play is, modestly but essentially, our creation as well as Shakespeare's and the actors'. In so doing, the Chorus poses a fundamental challenge for a television production of *Henry V*. Television, unlike the theater, has the technical ability to show us walled cities, tramping horses, and ships setting out to sea; it can film groups of men in such a way that on our screens we will accept them as armies in collision. Television's power to present actual objects or strikingly lifelike images of them has habituated us to viewing its programs as passive, not active, spectators—as consumers rather than co-creators of what we see and hear. The ultimate measure of the television production of *HenryV* is whether it transcends the medium's conventions and habits and engages us actively, so that, seeing "perspectively," we can be the creative audience for whom Shakespeare asks.

ANNOTATED BIBLIOGRAPHY

Berman, Ronald, ed. *Twentieth Century Interpretations of* Henry V. Englewood Cliffs, N.J.: Prentice-Hall, 1968.
This collection offers important and representative essays by various scholars and critics—some dealing with the background of the play, others offering interpretations and viewpoints.

Goddard, Harold C. "*Henry V.*" In his *The Meaning of Shakespeare*, pp. 215–68. Chicago: University of Chicago Press, 1951.
Goddard argues that in *Henry V* Shakespeare subtly but effectively undercuts his apparent portrait of Henry as ideal king and hero.

Goldman, Michael. "*Henry V:* The Strain of Rule." In his *Shakespeare and the Energies of Drama*, pp. 58–73. Princeton: Princeton University Press, 1972.
Goldman explores the relationship between the Chorus and the King, seeing both as speakers who summon their respective hearers to make extraordinary efforts.

Jorgens, Jack J. "Laurence Olivier's *Henry V.*" In his *Shakespeare on Film,* pp. 122–35. Bloomington and London: Indiana University Press, 1972.
Jorgens describes and analyzes what was, until the BBC-TV/Time-Life production of *Henry V,* the most widely seen version of the play.

Ornstein, Robert. *"Henry V."* In his *A Kingdom for the Stage: The Achievement of Shakespeare's History Plays,* pp. 175–202. Cambridge, Mass.: Harvard University Press, 1972.
Ornstein examines how, under the guise of naivete, Shakespeare has fashioned an artful meditation on the character and accomplishments of Henry V.

Rabkin, Norman. "Rabbits, Ducks, and *Henry V.*" *Shakespeare Quarterly* 28 (1977):279–96.
Rabkin sees *Henry V* as a work deliberately crafted so that it points in opposite directions, thus moving us to acknowledge how our own deepest hopes and fears about the realm of political action coexist in us.

Notes

1. So called because the plays in it were composed before those in the "second" tetralogy, which *Henry V* concludes.
2. See *Richard III,* I, iv, 42–65.
3. Note that Falstaff's calling Henry Jove anticipates how Exeter characterizes Henry to the French court: "Therefore in fierce tempest is he coming,/In thunder and in earthquake, like a Jove. . . ." (II, iv, 99–100).
4. I use "act" and "seems" because it is possible to play this scene so that either or both of the characters recognizes the other while pretending not to know him.
5. Note, too, that Falstaff had addressed Henry as "my heart" just before his rejection in the last act of 2 Henry IV (V, v, 47).
6. In Terry Hands' 1975 production of *Henry V* for the Royal Shakespeare Company, with Alan Howard as Henry, the shadows of dangling bodies plummeted into view and Henry turned to look at them as he spoke. In Laurence Olivier's 1944 film the camera shows us Falstaff dying as we hear Hostess Quickly's words voice-over.
7. The King James Version of Psalm 23 begins, "The Lord is my shepherd; I shall not want. He maketh me to lie down in green pastures. . . ."
8. On discovering that he is, like all men, mortal, Richard II declares:
Cover your heads, and mock not flesh and blood
With solemn reverence. Throw away respect,
Tradition, form, and ceremonious duty;
For you have but mistook me all this while.
I live with bread like you, feel want, taste grief,
Need friends. Subjected thus,
How can you say to me I am a king? (*Richard II,* III, ii, 171–77)
9. Stanley Wells, in his edition of *Richard II,* refers to this painting when discussing the use of the word *perspectives* in II, ii, 18. *Cf. Richard II,* New Penguin edition (Baltimore, Maryland: Penguin Books, 1969), p. 200.
10. Ironically, one effect of Henry's order requiring Pistol to kill his prisoner is that it deprives him of the ransom money that would have been legitimately his. Penniless except for Fluellen's grote, Pistol, who departed for France "the very blood to suck," vows to return to England and batten there instead: "Well, bawd, I'll turn,/And something lean to cutpurse of quick hand./To England will I steal, and there I'll steal" (V, i, 77–79).
11. It is possible that Williams refuses Henry's money as well as Fluellen's. If so, he is a man less easily pacified than his king.

SELF-TEST

Multiple-choice Questions

1. What offer does the French king make to King Henry to stop the war?
   a. his life
   b. the hand of his daughter Katherine and some unprofitable dukedoms
   c. financial aid to fight the other enemies of England
   d. he offers to restructure Salic law
   e. a goodly portion of the French treasury
2. Which of the following is *not* an example of how Shakespeare omitted or altered history for dramatic purposes?
   a. presentation of the King of France as a meek but competent ruler
   b. omission of major battles after the Battle of Agincourt
   c. condensation of about five years into one prologue
   d. presentation of the English defeating the French against overwhelming odds
   e. linking of the battle of Agincourt with the peace treaty that followed in the play
3. What do the Dauphin and Pistol have in common by the end of the play?
   a. Both are dead.
   b. Both learn that their loved one has died.
   c. Both are exposed as braggarts.
   d. Both have won honor on the battlefield.
   e. Both are seriously wounded.
4. Which of the following best expresses Henry's conception of the relationship between a king and his subjects?
   a. "If the king's cause be wrong, then the subject's obedience to the king wipes out the crime."
   b. "The king himself hath a heavy reckoning to make when he is called to answer for the souls of those who died in battle."
   c. "Every subject's duty is the king's, but every subject's soul is his own."
   d. "The better part of valor is discretion, in which the better part the king saves the subject's life."
   e. "Within the true king's duty lies the life and soul of each of his subjects."
5. On whose advice does King Henry most heavily depend before making the decision to go to France to fight?
   a. the clergy
   b. the House of Commons
   c. his former alehouse friends
   d. Scroop, Cambridge, and Grey
   e. God, through his personal prayers
6. How does the King receive the gift from the Dauphin?
   a. He treasures it and proclaims he will keep it always.
   b. Using eloquent puns, he vows to get even.
   c. He sends the gift back, unopened.
   d. He laughs good naturedly and asks that the messenger send his thanks to the Dauphin.
   e. He is dissapointed because he had expected more from the Dauphin.

7. What is the nature of King Henry's demand for surrender of the town of Harfleur?
   a. It is a gentle request that lives on both sides be spared.
   b. It is a stern admonition that many men will die in battle if Harfleur is not surrendered.
   c. It is a blood-thirsty threat of havoc, mayhem, rape, and pillage.
   d. It is a Christian appeal to Harfleur's moral sense of right and wrong.
   e. It is more of a plea than a demand that Henry not be forced to send Englishmen to a death in a foreign land for the sake of capturing a little-known town.
8. Of the following characters, who seems most aware of the true nature of the other alehouse characters?
   a. Bardolph
   b. Nym
   c. Pistol
   d. Boy
   e. Hostess (Nell)
9. Which of the following does *not* occur in the finale?
   a. Henry woos Katherine.
   b. The terms of peace are announced.
   c. The Queen of France delivers a speech on the blessings of peace.
   d. The matters of state are brought to a conclusion.
   e. Henry becomes the new ruler of France.
10. Match the persons listed in Column I with the perspectives on war listed in Column II.

    Column I
    _____ a. alehouse privates
    _____ b. English captains
    _____ c. King Henry
    _____ d. French noblemen
    _____ e. most soldiers and fighting men

    Column II
    1. a chance to compete and display valor
    2. a sport and a personal trial
    3. a vocation with certain rules and principles
    4. a moral duty
    5. a chance to steal and profit

Short-answer Essay Questions
1. Discuss the effects of Shakespeare's decision to begin the events of the play with the discussion between the Archbishop of Canterbury and the Bishop of Ely.
2. Why is "Boy" in the play?
3. Discuss the different uses to which Henry puts his powers of eloquence.
4. What justification does Henry give for his order to slay the French prisoners? In what ways is this supported or undermined by the play itself?
5. What are the functions of the choruses (including Prologue and Epilogue) in *Henry V*?

Questions for Reflection
1. What are the roles and functions of the women who appear in *Henry V,* a play centered on the martial exploits of its hero?
2. Why is Act V in the play? How does it alter our conception of what has preceded it?

3. Especially in the first two acts, Henry is described as a man who has changed radically. Discuss whether Henry does or does not continue to change during the course of the play.
4. Discuss how the television production of *Henry V* changes Shakespeare's text and in so doing alters our perception of Henry and of the major issues being addressed in the play.
5. Why does Henry V really go to war in France? If his claim to the French throne is genuine, why doesn't he assume it after Agincourt? What other motives are suggested by the play?

ANSWER KEY

Answers to Multiple-choice Questions
1. a (III, ii)
2. d (essay)
3. c (essay)
4. c (essay, and IV, i)
5. a (I, ii)
6. b (I, ii)
7. c (III, iii)
8. d (II, iii)
9. e (V, ii)
10. a: 5 (essay)
    b: 3 (essay)
    c: 2 (essay)
    d: 1 (essay)
    e: 4 (essay)

Suggested Answers to Short-answer Essay Questions
1. While much of their conversation is expository—they discuss the marvelous transformation Henry has made from dissolute prince to statesmanlike king—they also discuss a bill pending before the Commons that would confiscate most of the Church's secular property. In the view of the two prelates, encouraging Henry's interest in acquiring the French domains to which he believes he has legitimate claim would assuage his apparent need to acquire real estate while at the same time diverting his attention from church property. Considering the fact that Shakespeare could have used his opportunity to discuss the intricacies of the Salic law, upon which Henry was basing the moral rectitude of his legal claim to France, the opening dialogue actually serves to complicate the audience's perception of the royal hero of the play. It raises the whole issue of why Henry really wanted to go to war, a controversy that is never answered definitively in the play.
2. The only serious, reliable person among the comic "underworld" cluster of characters in the play, Boy's personal integrity contrasts sharply with the degeneracy of his patrons: Nym, Bardolph, and Pistol. He protests his worth, condemns the immorality of the others, and determines to leave his companions in an eloquent soliloquy in III, ii, 25–49. As the play progresses, Boy's integrity perseveres while the camaraderie of what's left of Falstaff's old "tavern crowd" disintegrates. Boy serves a number of other functions: (a) In IV, iv, his fluency in French enables Pistol to engage in a comic dialogue with a French nobleman during the battle;

(b) in the same scene, Boy forewarns the audience of the vulnerability of the English camp to a French flank attack; (c) the ensuing death of this innocent youth in the unjustifiable carnage by the French not only illustrates the inherent horror of war but also heightens the audience's anger at the cowardly deed; and (d) the audience's emotional response to Boy's death may serve partially—but only partially—to relieve Henry of a measure of the blame he must receive for ordering the slaughter of the helpless French prisoners, an act of comparable villainy.

3. Examples of the uses to which Henry puts his powers of eloquence include the following five situations: (1) Henry is eloquent when he wishes to chastise people as he does the French ambassador for the Dauphin's impudent reply to Henry's claim to certain French dukedoms (I, ii, 260–98), as he does the three traitors—Scroop, Cambridge, and Grey—and condemns them to death, and as he does Montjoy for the Constable of France's offer not to fight if Henry gives himself up for ransom. (2) He is eloquent when he wishes to exhort English soldiers and noblemen in preparation for battle, as he does just prior to the siege of Harfleur (III, i, 1–34). In reproving Westmoreland for complaining about the paucity of English soldiers facing the French at Agincourt, Henry maintains that the honor and glory that will be earned in the forthcoming battle will be the more precious and coveted for the small numbers that will be able to claim it (IV, iii, 18–67). (3) Henry is also eloquent when he warns the French of the consequences of their temerity in opposing the English forces, as he does before the walls of Harfleur (III, iii, 1–43) and to Montjoy who carries a message from the King of France threatening revenge for the fall of Harfleur (III, vi, 133–65). (4) He is eloquent when he discusses or soliloquizes on the responsibilities and burdens of kingship. In a dialogue with some English soldiers, Henry maintains that while subjects owe allegiance to their king and his causes, they cannot use this allegiance to absolve themselves of all moral responsibility for their individual actions (IV, i, 139–75). In a later soliloquy, Henry bemoans the chronic insomnia of royalty burdened with the cares of office. (5) Finally, Henry waxes eloquent when he woos and proposes to his intended bride, Katherine (V, ii, 132–65, 214–38).

4. At the moment he ordered the slaughter of the French prisoners, Henry's stated reason was the news that the French were reinforcing their troops. (IV, vi, 35–38). Immediately preceding this, the Duke of Exeter had described to Henry the valiant battlefield deaths of the Earl of Suffolk and the Duke of York. Shakespeare provides no soliloquy at this juncture in which Henry might have agonized over the moral dilemma; consequently, we must assume his order was given as an expediency. Henry subsequently restates his rationale for the slaughter: a justifiable retaliation for the French slaughter of innocent boys and servants in the English camp (IV, viii, 50–60); moreover, Gower and Fluellen, in discussing events of the battle, also suggest that Henry's order was retaliatory (IV, vii, 1–10). But Shakespeare sees to it that Henry learns of the dastardly French deed *after* he has ordered the murder of the French; consequently, Henry's revised excuses are made to sound specious.

5. In the tradition of Greek theatre, the chorus usually provided a periodic, running commentary on the events and themes dealt with in the play. In *Henry V,* Shakespeare provides a Chorus at the beginning of each act. Among the functions the Chorus serves are (1) to apologize to the audience for the deficiencies of the stage

as a setting for the play (I, Pro., 8–14); (2) to describe events occurring between acts (I, Pro., 28–30 and III, Cho., 28–33); (3) to bridge over time and space (V, Cho., 3–6); (4) to warn of events yet to come (II, Cho., 20–30); and (5) to ask the members of the audience to use their imaginations to depict settings and events not portrayable on stage (III, Cho.). The Epilogue, rather than summing up, presages some of the events that will occur during the reign of Henry's son, Henry VI, that have their roots in the play just concluded.

THE TEMPEST

INTRODUCTION TO THE PLAY

Written around 1611, *The Tempest* is probably one of Shakespeare's last two plays. It is among his shortest and, by many accounts, is one of his best. It is also the only play in which Shakespeare faithfully adheres to the dramatic unities of time, place, and action called for in the classical Greek tradition. You may have to remind yourself, after you have finished reading or watching *The Tempest*, that despite the play's many and varied events, the entire action occurs during the course of a single afternoon and in a single locale. Some scholars feel that Shakespeare, who systematically ignored these theoretical dramatic conventions in his other plays, recognized them but once, in *The Tempest*, as a contemptuous parting shot at his orthodox critics.

In addition to following the guidelines of classical drama, *The Tempest* also falls comfortably into the category of medieval and Renaissance drama known as the "romances" or "tragicomedies." While neither term is wholly descriptive of *The Tempest*, "romance" stems from the fact that the storyline is usually a farfetched fantasy with love as its central concern. In *The Tempest*, the lovers are Ferdinand and Miranda, of course. Events and situations are wildly improbable and there is little or no regard for the rules of everyday causality. Much of the play deals with illusion—the opening storm, the vanishing banquet, music from an invisible source—and the play's characters include a supernatural magician, a beast-slave, an "airy spirit" (Ariel), and various and sundry other minor spirits and nymphs. Yet, while events and situations are improbable, the emotions and attitudes of the characters in *The Tempest* are real enough, and rational. The "comic" aspect of this type of play stems from the fact that it ends happily. Yet the play includes themes and elements that are potentially disastrous, hence the "tragic" title. In *The Tempest*, these potentially tragic elements include Caliban's attempted rape of Miranda, Caliban's plot to stab Prospero, and Antonio and Sebastian's conspiracy to kill Alonso and Gonzalo. These real and malevolent events serve as intrusions on the benevolent fantasy and remind the audience of the baser aspects of human nature.

The reader may wish to take some time to remember who's who in *The Tempest*, a task Shakespeare has made difficult by selecting an overabundance of masculine names ending in either "o" (Alonso, Prospero, Antonio, Gonzalo, Trinculo, Stephano, Francisco) or "an" (Sebastian, Adrian, Caliban). The only exceptions among his major characters are Ferdinand, Miranda, and Ariel. The reader should also understand that most of the events that motivate the characters in *The Tempest* took place some twelve years before the time of the play itself: the usurpation of Prospero's dukedom by his brother Angelo; Prospero's banishment to sea in a leaky boat with his infant daughter, Miranda; Prospero and Miranda's arrival at the enchanted island populated by the man-beast Caliban, offspring of the witch Sycorax, who has herself spellbound the spirit Ariel; and Prospero's assumption of control of the island and its spirits by his superior magical talents.

While students and critics of Shakespeare seldom agree on the ultimate meaning or relative importance of the themes in a play by that playwright (nor should we expect such agreement), some clear and coherent strands do emerge from the action of *The Tempest*. And you may wish to note these and follow them in your reading and viewing. These will be only briefly identified in this introduction, particularly as Joan Hartwig deals at some length with two of these themes in her essay; the remainder should challenge your independent observations.

One of the themes Hartwig considers is the way in which many characters and events parallel and parody each other throughout the play. Hartwig also discusses the theme of sin, trial, atonement, and reconciliation that most of the major characters in the play undergo. Shakespeare appears to have a special fondness for the potential of the younger generation (Ferdinand and Miranda) to overcome, through their innocence and faith in humanity, the evil that men of the older generation do one another as a result of their ambition and greed.

You may also wish to take note of the continuing contrast between illusion and reality presented throughout the play. From the opening storm, which turns out to be illusory, Shakespeare challenges his audience to determine which events and people are real and which are illusory. As an example, Antonio, who currently holds the title of Duke of Milan, is actually the usurper, while Prospero, who has been banished, is the "real" duke.

Shakespeare is also continually contrasting nature and society in *The Tempest,* as he often does in other plays. Caliban is a "creature of nature," innocent of the ways of society and therefore brutish, degenerate, and undisciplined. Still, he is not calculatingly and coldbloodedly evil in the way of Antonio, who, although one of the "civilized" characters of the play, nevertheless plots with Sebastian to take the life of Alonso. What, then, is Shakespeare trying to say about the values of civilization and raw nature, and the kinds of persons each has produced?

LESSON ASSIGNMENTS

In order to get the most out of the specially designed introductory material and to appreciate the unique qualities of the play itself, Joan Hartwig strongly recommends that you prepare yourself in the following manner:
- Read the synopsis of *The Tempest* in this guide.
- Read the text of *The Tempest*.
- Read "*The Tempest*: Parallels and Parodies" by Joan Hartwig in this guide.
- View the television production.
- Complete the Self-test at the end of this lesson.

LEARNING OBJECTIVES

After completing the reading assignments and viewing the televised drama production, you should be able to:
1. Identify and analyze parallels in the ways characters respond to and act in analogous situations.
2. Distinguish between Prospero the magician and Prospero the man.
3. Describe the personality and role of Caliban and analyze how he parodies, or is parodied by, other characters in the play.
4. Describe how Shakespeare shifts the audience's perspective and integrates the audience into the play's action.
5. Identify the trial each character must undergo in order to achieve a place in the final reconciliation, and describe the effect of each trial on the character experiencing it.

SYNOPSIS OF THE PLAY

ACT I

Somewhere in the Mediterranean Sea, a raging storm threatens to sink the ship bearing ALONSO, the King of Naples; ANTONIO, the Duke of Milan; and their followers. From a nearby island, the sorcerer PROSPERO and his daughter, MIRANDA, watch. Distressed, Miranda pleads with her father to use his powers to end the tempest. He tells her that no one has been harmed, and explains to Miranda how they came to the island: Twelve years earlier, Prospero, then the Duke of Milan, was deposed by his brother, Antonio. He and Miranda were set adrift in a leaky boat, but a courtier named GONZALO hid food and drink aboard and they reached the island safely. Now fate has brought Prospero's enemies to his shores.

Prospero puts Miranda to sleep and summons his servant, ARIEL, a spirit of the air. Ariel tells him that the ship is safe and its passengers dispersed about the island, each group thinking that the others have drowned.

Prospero awakens Miranda and they visit their beast-slave, CALIBAN. Prospero orders Caliban to gather firewood. Roaring and grumbling, he obeys.

Meanwhile, Ariel, with an enchanted song, lures FERDINAND, the son of King Alonso, to a place where Miranda can see him. Other than her father, Ferdinand is the first man Miranda has seen, and they fall in love at first sight. Prospero pretends to oppose the romance and enslaves Ferdinand.

ACT II

The second act introduces King Alonso and his party, who are mourning the supposed death of Prince Ferdinand. Invisible, Ariel lulls all to sleep except Prospero's evil brother, Antonio, and the King's brother, SEBASTIAN. Antonio convinces Sebastian to murder the King and become king himself; but Ariel wakens the sleepers just in time.

Elsewhere on the island, Caliban meets TRINCULO, the King's jester, and STEPHANO, the King's drunken butler. Soon all three are drunk with wine, and Caliban falls down and worships Stephano as a god.

ACT III

Miranda comforts Ferdinand, who is exhausted from carrying logs. Hidden, Prospero is pleased to hear them pledge their love.

Meanwhile, Caliban urges Stephano and Trinculo to kill Prospero and rule the island, with Stephano taking Miranda as his wife. Ariel, who has heard every word, lures them astray with music.

Elsewhere, the King's party is amazed at the appearance of an enchanted banquet. Suddenly, the banquet vanishes and Ariel delivers a fiery sermon on their sins. Deeply moved, King Alonso rushes off in despair.

ACT IV

Convinced of their true love, Prospero pledges Miranda to Ferdinand, and stages a magical spectacle to celebrate their engagement. He breaks it off suddenly, however, to deal with Caliban and his would-be assassins. When the drunken trio arrives, they are driven off by spirits summoned by Ariel.

ACT V

Ariel compassionately describes the plight of Prospero's enemies, and the magician vows to forgive them, explaining the strange things that have occurred. Finally, he vows to renounce his magic and return to Milan with them. Before casting off his enchanted robes forever, he releases Ariel to the winds and Caliban from his enslavement.

In the Epilogue, Prospero confirms that his magic powers are gone and asks the audience to receive the play with applause.

The Tempest: **Parallels and Parodies**

Joan Hartwig

The Tempest is a fantasy, full of wondrous creatures and supernatural events, which are controlled by the supreme magician Prospero. Yet simply because the play suspends reality, we should not expect it to ignore the conventional devices of dramatic construction. The play not only employs these devices but is, in fact, a fine example of how they can be employed in creating a tightly knit and precisely balanced play.

A principal dramatic device Shakespeare employs in *The Tempest* is parallel. Parallels of characters, actions, thoughts, emotions, and events abound, the sides of each parallel serving to illuminate each other. Some of these parallels are straightforward, as we shall see, but Shakespeare has refined many of them into finely wrought parodies.

The parallels are with us from the very beginning of the play. Master manipulator of the audience that he was, Shakespeare draws the audience immediately into the parallels, as well as the fantasy of the play, by making the audience experience dislocations of perspective similar to those being experienced by the characters themselves.

As the play opens, we witness what we assume to be a natural storm, with an actual ship and its passengers being wracked by the winds and high seas. The Boatswain's brusqueness as he cuts through the superficialities of social and political rank to give orders—"To cabin! Silence! Trouble us not!" (I, i, 15–16)—and Gonzalo's good-natured description of the Boatswain as a man better fit for death on the gallows than by drowning, together with the bustle of activity and the "wet Mariners," indicate a natural event. The audience thus finds itself initially in the midst of the action. Yet in the very next moment, we are pulled to a more distant view as Miranda describes how she saw the ship sink into the sea, bemoaning the loss of such a "brave vessel" and the people within it. Then Prospero assures her that the storm was the result of his magic powers and that no one has been harmed. Not long after, while Miranda sleeps, we learn from Ariel that he *was* the storm, flaming here and there about the ship (I, ii, 195ff.). If we had felt assured at the play's beginning that our ordinary way of looking at "reality" was adequate for this play, by now we have probably changed our minds. The audience therefore undergoes a dislocation of its perceived reality in almost as crucial a way as do the characters from the ship.

After these initial dislocations of perceived reality, Shakespeare moves to have his audience adopt a balanced view of the events that are to transpire. When Gonzalo and his King, Alonso, together with the King's brother Sebastian and Prospero's brother Antonio, find themselves in surroundings totally foreign to them, having unexpectedly survived what seemed certain death in the shipwreck, they converse and attempt to evaluate their "new" condition. Gonzalo sees the island's properties as "lush and lusty," whereas Antonio finds them "tawny" (II, i, 52–53)—each according to the perspective he ordinarily employs to view what is outside himself. Gonzalo's cheerful positive vision and Antonio's disparaging negativity polarize each other and, by so doing, encourage the audience to balance its own view somewhere in between.[1]

Not only do the characters and the audience from the "old" world have to adjust to unfamiliar circumstances, Caliban and Miranda must find a way to see without distortion the new occupants of their island. Neither has ever seen beings other than themselves, Caliban's "dam" Sycorax, and Prospero; thus, their experience has not prepared them for encounters with these wondrous creatures from another world. Miranda's response to Ferdinand when she first sees him—"I might call him/A thing divine; for nothing natural/I ever saw so noble" (I, ii, 418–20)—closely parallels Caliban's response to Stephano and Trinculo—"These be fine things, an if they be not sprites./ That's a brave god [Stephano] and bears celestial liquor . . . Thou wondrous man" (II, ii, 114–15; 160). Each point of view is tempered, one by Prospero's evaluation of Ferdinand—"To th' most of men this is a Caliban,/And they to him are angels" (I, ii, 481–82)—and the other by Trinculo's comments on Caliban's credulity—"A most ridiculous monster, to make a wonder of a poor drunkard!" (II, ii, 161–62).

Miranda's adoration of such a noble creature might win our approval, because romantic convention dictates that "love at first sight" is acceptable. And we might therefore think Prospero an unnecessarily difficult and disapproving father when he belittles the love-match to their faces and demands that Ferdinand pass some tests of his "virtue." Certainly Miranda thinks her father excessive in requiring Ferdinand to carry logs like a slave. And Miranda's simplicity of adoration for Ferdinand is paralleled, and parodied, by Caliban's unquestioning adoption of Stephano as his "new master." This parallel is but one of many in *The Tempest* that Shakespeare intensifies through the use of parody.

The function of parody[2] is more complex than travesty or burlesque in that it not only causes us to see the "serious" action replayed in comically reduced terms; it also asks us to rethink both actions in light of each other's values. Most often, those values, held as absolutes at either end of a spectrum, undergo important modifications because of their parallel relationship.

The modern word *parody* has its roots in a Greek word (*parode*) that means a song sung beside or against. Modern usage understands parody to ridicule that which it imitates, reducing the original to literal and usually demeaning proportions. Despite the narrowing of the term's meaning in this century, however, I would distinguish between *parody* and *burlesque*. *Burlesque* draws in and limits meaning to its proportions, whereas *parody,* after the initial reduction, leads out of itself and lends a fresh perspective on that which it imitates, as Shakespeare so skillfully demonstrates throughout *The Tempest.*

Caliban provides parody of several characters—Miranda and Ferdinand as examples—and situations throughout the play. He is like Miranda in his ignorance of the world outside their island, and so his responses, like hers, are innocent. Yet his nature, unlike hers, is base, and he is attracted to baseness in Stephano, the drunken butler, and Trinculo, the drunken jester. Miranda, whose name designates her wonderful beauty and perfection (as Ferdinand reminds us [III, i, 37–39]), is attracted to like nobility and beauty in Ferdinand. Yet, if we disregard the "call" of like-to-like natures, we see that Caliban and Miranda are basically similar, responding without experience and in ignorance, and both might easily be misled.

To further increase our recognition of the similarities between Caliban and Ferdinand, but always within the measure of parody, Shakespeare draws several marked parallels. One such parallel is the potential lust of both Caliban and Ferdinand for Miranda and the actions Prospero takes to ensure the containment of their lust.[3] Caliban's initial appearance reminds Miranda what a beast this being is. When Prospero tells her that "We'll visit Caliban," she responds, " 'Tis a villain, sir,/I do not love to look on" (I, ii, 308–10). Prospero insists that Caliban must be considered, nonetheless, because he performs services that make their existence more comfortable. In their ensuing exchange, Prospero recalls how, after caring for Caliban as his own child and lodging him in his "cell," Caliban repaid him by trying to rape his daughter. Caliban's laughing recollection tells us that for him the violation of Miranda's virginity is insignificant, but it is a point that Prospero later makes deliberately significant as he speaks to Ferdinand. Then Miranda recalls how she tried to teach Caliban language and he jests that "my profit on't/Is, I know how to curse" (I, ii, 363–64).

Recalcitrant and unregenerate, Caliban leaves the stage at the same moment that Ferdinand enters. This visual pairing of Caliban and Ferdinand brings them into parallel focus not only for the audience but also for Miranda, who cannot help but see the vast difference between the two. Enhanced thus, Ferdinand appears as "a thing divine," which makes Prospero's denigrating comparison between him and Caliban (I, ii, 481–82) seem entirely unreasonable. In addition, there is Prospero's accusation that Ferdinand is a "traitor," having "put thyself/Upon this island as a spy, to win it/From me, the lord on 't" (I, ii, 455–57). Prospero lets the audience know, of course, that his negative reaction to Ferdinand is a role he invents to test the Prince's nature, and the audience also knows that such a charge is contrary to fact. But note another parallel. Caliban has already charged Prospero with taking the island from him (I, ii, 331–44) and later makes a similar claim to Stephano and Trinculo—"A sorcerer, that by his cunning hath/Cheated me of the island" (III, ii, 42–43). Prospero, in this case, provides a parody of Caliban's accusations when he wrongly accuses Ferdinand of treason, and this parody encourages us to discount Caliban's claims as we do Prospero's, realizing that each speaker alters the facts to suit his purposes of the moment.

Visual parallels between Caliban and Ferdinand occur in II, ii and III, i, successive scenes that begin with Caliban carrying "a burden of wood" and Ferdinand "bearing a log." Both characters discuss the terms of their servitude grudgingly, Caliban cursing Prospero and Ferdinand noting that only Miranda's presence "makes my labors pleasures" (III, i, 7). Their different attitudes toward Prospero's imposed authority are made clearer because their physical, visible actions are the same. Similarly, their common acceptance of slavery leads us to see a crucial difference. Ferdinand, whose nature is to rule, accepts slavery because of his love for Miranda:

The very instant that I saw you, did
My heart fly to your service; there resides,
To make me slave to it; and for your sake
Am I this patient log-man.

(III, i, 64–67)

Caliban proves that he is by nature a slave when he encounters Stephano and determines to cast off Prospero's authority in order to subject himself to his new "god": "I'll kiss thy foot. I'll swear myself thy subject" (II, ii, 148).

The two are paired also in their praise of Miranda's beauty. In order to reach the conclusion that Miranda is "so perfect and so peerless," Ferdinand admits that he has known "full many a lady," and that "many a time/Th' harmony of their tongues hath into bondage/Brought my too diligent ear" (III, i, 39–42). Caliban, in contrast, "never saw a woman/But only Sycorax my dam and she;/But she as far surpasseth Sycorax/As great'st does least" (III, ii, 97–100). Each is aware of Miranda's superior beauty but one speaks out of prior knowledge of this world's beauties and the other out of ignorance. Ferdinand speaks hoping to win Miranda's love for himself, whereas Caliban is pandering to Stephano's lust, setting up a breeder-queen to people the island once Prospero is dead. The contrast between the motives of lover and pimp creates different effects in the descriptions of Miranda's beauty, but their external similarities encourage us to see beyond the present moment with Prospero's prescience and to realize the danger of lust that could mar the perfect union between the lovers and stain the generations to come.

This theme of ideal love marred by lust is central to the masque that Prospero presents to celebrate the betrothal of his daughter and Ferdinand. Iris the rainbow calls upon Ceres, the goddess of plenty, to bless this nuptial, but Ceres wants to be sure that Venus and her son Cupid will have no part in the ceremony. As Ceres says, she is mistrustful of those two ever since they abetted in abducting her daughter Proserpine to join Dis, the god of the underworld, for a third of each year. Iris assures Ceres that Venus and Cupid will not be present, although they did have a plot, since broken,

> to have done
> Some wanton charm upon this man and maid,
> Whose vows are, that no bed-right shall be paid
> Till Hymen's torch be lighted.
>
> (IV, i, 94–97)

With such assurance that lust will not mar the ceremony, the masque proceeds, only to be interrupted when Prospero remembers "that foul conspiracy/Of the beast Caliban and his confederates/Against my life" (IV, i, 139–41). Once more the figure of lust intrudes upon the harmonious celebration of love's ideal perfection.

Prospero needs to remain alert in order to contain Caliban's threats to deter the fulfillment of his purposes. This has not always come naturally to him. In the past, he was forced to learn the need to be alert, when Caliban attempted to violate Miranda. Earlier, he learned of his brother's treachery only when he was ousted from his dukedom. The fact that Caliban is replaying, with less subtlety and more directly intended violence, the pre-play usurpation, is another instance of his parodic function. Prospero describes Antonio's usurpation in I, ii, when he tells Miranda the heretofore secret history of their journey of exile (the audience learns at the same time that Miranda learns what she has often wondered about but was never privileged to know—a clever expository device that increases the audience's identification with the play's action). Antonio and Sebastian replay that plot in their thwarted attempt to kill Alonso and Gonzalo (II, i), and Caliban plays it yet again in his recruiting of Stephano and Trinculo to kill Prospero and gain control of the island. The repetitions of the original crime occur in the play's present action in comically contained forms. Sebastian must have a final word with Antonio *after* they have drawn their swords, and Stephano and Trinculo must try on the deceptively glittering clothes before they proceed (much to Caliban's distress). In each instance, Prospero has Ariel ready to ensure that the plots will not be realized, but in each case the characters themselves provide their own crucial delays because of comic pendantry and comic vanity. In effect, the usurpation/regicide plot is reduced from evil threat to farcical inertia, and this parodic reduction allows the villainous plotters to be included in the play's final harmonious vision, despite the fact that not all of them are repentent.[4]

Yet another instance of Caliban's function as the focus of comedy may be seen in the surprised reactions of Ferdinand and of Stephano that these "natives" of the island can speak their own language. Ferdinand is already charmed by Miranda's beauty, thinking her a "goddess," and when she answers his question whether she "be a maid or no" in his language, he is overwhelmed (I, ii, 422–29). When Stephano stumbles over Caliban, under whose gaberdine Trinculo has hidden from the storm, and Caliban cries out, Stephano likewise is surprised: "Where the devil should he learn our language?" (II, ii, 65–66). Not only does Caliban speak, but when Trinculo recognizes the other voice as Stephano's, he calls out, and Stephano is further astonished: "Four legs and two voices—a most delicate monster!" (II, ii, 88–89). Thus, what appears in Ferdinand as sublime wonder is broadened under Stephano's response to comic absurdity. The two attitudes, so similar to begin with, collide against each other because of the disparity between the objects that generate them. Upon recognition of the analogy, however, each modifies the other.[5]

Parallels of action occur many times, several of which involve Caliban, as we have seen, and some of which do not. Various characters draw their swords, for example, and are unable to act thereafter. The most intriguing impotence occurs when Sebastian and Antonio have raised their swords to kill Alonso and Gonzalo and then Sebastian thinks of something else he must talk over (II, i, 291). This might be seen as a parodic imitation of the spellbound actors: Ferdinand in I, ii, who raises his sword to protest Prospero's control over him, and the several members of Alonso's court party who raise their swords against Ariel's Harpy presence when he banishes the magic banquet (III, iii, 67–68). The two instances on either side of II, i are obviously magic truncations of intended acts, but in the middle stands that resonant human twitch that delays the moment of effective action beyond repair.

Another parallel is found in Ariel's songs throughout the play and Caliban's song in Act II, scene ii.[6] Ariel charms the characters with his music: His song leads Ferdinand from his bankside grieving—"This music crept by me upon the waters,/Allaying both their fury and my passion/With its sweet air" (I, ii, 392–94). He both encourages Alonso and Gonzalo to fall into their recuperating sleep and awakens Gonzalo to ward off the assassination attempt of Sebastian and Antonio (II, i, s.d, 198; s.d., 292ff.). He also is the cause of Caliban's remarkable speech describing the "sounds and sweet airs that give delight and hurt not" (III, ii, s.d., 121; 132ff.). He even entrances that drunken trio—Caliban, Stephano, and Trinculo—into following his music (III, ii), although they are put off by his invisibility. The picture of Ariel's leading them off the stage, following his music, contrasts markedly with the preceding scene (II, ii) in which a drunken Caliban leads Stephano and Trinculo off with his cacophonous song about freedom.

Sebastian and Antonio's delay parodically demonstrates the truth of Prospero's monitory prediction to Miranda:

I find my zenith doth depend upon
A most auspicious star, whose influence

> *If now I court not, but omit, my fortunes*
> *Will ever after droop.*
>
> (I, ii, 181–84)

Seizing the propitious moment for action is something Prospero has had to learn. His exile from Milan was due in part to his having neglected responsibility, allowing Antonio to take over his active duties as duke while he retired with his books, suiting his private preference (I, ii, 89ff.). Following his repair of society's broken order through the reconciliation of all the characters at play's end, he promises to "drown [his] book" (V, i, 57) and return to his life as rightful Duke of Milan. In order to achieve this "rarer action," however, Prospero has had to grow; in fact, he has had to undergo a transformation something like that of the other characters whom he controls.

The transformations experienced by most of the characters and the many and varied trials they endure before the final reconciliation constitute another—and major—group of parallels in the play. Alonso thinks he has lost his son, and grieves for him. Gonzalo attempts to comfort him with various diversions of the imagination, including his famous "commonwealth" speech (II, i, 143–64), but Alonso refuses to be comforted. Sebastian and Antonio, on the other hand, taunt Alonso with the fact that "the fault's your own" (II, i, 131). Gonzalo himself experiences loss primarily because his king is lost, and he cannot find himself until Alonso does. Even when the court group undergoes Ariel's accusations and magic spells, Gonzalo is exempt because he was not guilty of exiling Prospero. Nonetheless, his compassion for his companions leaves him with tears streaming down his face (V, i, 15–16; 63–64). Like Gonzalo, Francisco and Adrian, the almost silent courtiers, are guiltless themselves, but they must suffer because they are with the others. Sebastian and Antonio are the guiltiest, yet they feel the pangs of conscience least. They are forced to confront their guilt when Ariel, the Harpy, calls them and Alonso "three men of sin" (III, iii, 53), but they are noticeably unrepentant at the play's end. That all do suffer in Prospero's magic spell is clear from the description Prospero gives before he releases them from it: "A solemn air, and the best comforter/To an unsettled fancy, cure thy brains,/ Now useless, boiled within thy skull!" (V, i, 58–60).

Like Alonso, Ferdinand grieves because he assumes his father is dead, but more important to the action of the play, he undergoes a trial to prove that his love deserves Miranda. He is forced to demean himself and carry wood like a slave, as well as to bear the burden of Prospero's apparent disapproval. Miranda, too, though she would freely give herself to Ferdinand, must wait for Ferdinand to win her father's approval. Caliban, who provides a counterpoint to both Ferdinand and Miranda, must bear various pains that Prospero inflicts to keep him under control, but finally, and perhaps his greatest trial, is the lack of diligence and control he discovers in his newly found "god" and conspirators. With his self-appointed new master and the jester Trinculo, he must endure the spell in the "filthy mantled pool" (IV, i, 182) where Stephano and Trinculo lose their bottles (the worst fate they could imagine, no doubt). They emerge smelling of "horse-piss," and they steal the "glistering apparel" (IV, i, s.d., 193), only to be pursued by "spirits in shape of dogs and hounds" (IV, i, s.d., 253) that Prospero instructs to "grind their joints/With dry convulsions, shorten up their sinews/With aged cramps" (IV, i, 257–59). Clearly, theirs is a physical rather than a mental torment: The punishment suits their natures, which are primarily concerned with physical indulgences.

Even the Master, the Boatswain, and the Mariners suffer in that they think their ship is actually splitting. At the end, of course, they are returned after having been refreshed by spell-wrought sleep; and they are able to rejoice in the restoration of their "yare" ship and the safety of their king and company.

Ariel, the spirit neither human nor inhuman, may seem to be beyond pain as he changes identity with whimsical dexterity. But Prospero has to remind him of the twelve years he suffered under Sycorax's spell, confined in a "cloven pine," in order to keep Ariel from rebelling against doing "more toil" (I, ii, 242). Prospero even has to threaten like punishment— "I will rend an oak/And peg thee in his knotty entrails" (I, ii, 294–95)—if Ariel complains further. Ariel, like Caliban, wants to be free of Prospero's mastery, but unlike Caliban, Ariel understands that willing servitude wins rewards. It is for the promise of release, finally, that Ariel does his chores. Having accepted Prospero's terms, Ariel capitulates his will with grace and enthusiasm: "That's my noble master!/What shall I do? Say what? What shall I do?" (I, ii, 299–300).

Prospero's trial is one of giving up control, of accepting human limitations once more, even of accepting his failure with Caliban.[7] "This thing of darkness I/Acknowledge mine" (V, i, 275–76) is an admission that, despite his magic powers and his humane efforts, Prospero could not "nurture" Caliban's corrupt "nature." Caliban surprises him, however, in the final scene by recognizing Prospero as his true master and by promising to reform.

> *I'll be wise hereafter,*
> *And seek for grace. What a thrice-double ass*
> *Was I to take this drunkard for a god*
> *And worship this dull fool!*
>
> (V, i, 295–98)

It is likely that Prospero is more stunned by this unanticipated "conversion" than is the audience, even though his gruff, "go to! Away!" does not necessarily indicate that.

Prospero's trial is also an act of release, of giving up those things that have been dear to him. It is, for example, at least as difficult for him to release

Ariel as it is for him to break his magic staff and drown his magic book. The sometimes-harsh Prospero gives a touching response to Ariel's song in Act V, scene i: "Why, that's my dainty Ariel! I shall miss thee" (V, i, 95). Together with an earlier question, "Do you love me, master? No?, "and Prospero's answer, "Dearly, my delicate Ariel" (IV, i, 48–49), this sign of Prospero's gentle feelings indicates that he too is but human.

Along the way, Prospero has shown several responses that integrate him into the level of human characters despite his superior magic powers. In his first scene, he repeatedly nudges Miranda to rivet her attention upon his narration, even when she swears that she is hanging on his every word. This device may be calculated by Shakespeare to nudge the theater audience to attention more than Miranda, but within the play's terms of characterization, it also suggests that Prospero is more than a little vain about his skills as a teacher and a storyteller. In addition, his need to take advantage of the moment that has been provided for him to carry out his design recognizes that he is not all-powerful, but rather is dependent upon a higher control (I, ii, 178–84). He unquestionably imitates that higher power in his mastery of the island's creatures, but he should not be identified as that power. Whenever he lays aside his magic robe, as he does in the expository scene with Miranda (I, ii, 23–25), he stands only as a man. As such, he is capable of an ordinary sense of humor, displayed in his jest when Miranda questions whether he is her father, if her father was Duke of Milan: Prospero jokes, "Thy mother was a piece of virtue, and/She said thou wast my daughter" (I, ii, 56–57). He is also capable of emotions, as he displays in his sudden anger against both Caliban and Ariel when they attempt rebellion; and he forgets. He becomes so intrigued with the art of his masque that he momentarily forgets the "foul conspiracy" of Caliban and the others upon his life. Prospero's agitation at this point is so intense that both Ferdinand and Miranda are startled by it. "Never till this day," Miranda says, "saw I him touched with anger so distempered" (IV, i, 144–45). Prospero immediately reassures them that he is once more in control and removes himself in order to still his "beating mind." With Ariel as his instrument, Prospero devises a plan to outwit Caliban and his confederates, but for that brief moment we are allowed to see into the extraordinary alertness and control that his mastery involves.

Prospero's final change from magician to man occurs when he takes off his magic robe and puts on his ducal clothing. He then forgives the sinners, without Antonio's repentance, for their crimes against Prospero, the man. And he releases his "delicate Ariel." His final gesture, the Epilogue, completes his transformation.[8]

> *Now my charms are all o'erthrown,*
> *And what strength I have's mine own,*
> *Which is most faint. Now, 'tis true*

I must be here confined by you,
Or sent to Naples.

(Epil., 1–5)

The ultimate control of all his efforts now depends upon the audience. We are given the greatest compliment he (and Shakespeare) can make. The powerful magician submits his will to our imagination, and only our approval and participation can release him from his bonds of service. The play's last parallel of action is to give the audience the power and the understanding of the magician.

ANNOTATED BIBLIOGRAPHY

NOTE: In addition to those works cited in the footnotes, I recommend reading the following:

Kay, Carol McGinnis, and Jacobs, Henry E., eds. *Shakespeare's Romances Reconsidered.* Lincoln and London: University of Nebraska Press, 1978.
This collection of papers read at the Alabama Symposium on Shakespeare in 1975 includes essays by Northrop Frye and Clifford Leech. Essays by Howard Felperin, Cyrus Hoy, Joan Hartwig, Charles Forker, and David Young are specifically concerned with *The Tempest*. Includes an excellent "selected" bibliography.

Kermode, Frank, ed. *The Tempest.* Arden Shakespeare Series. London: Methuen Inc., 1954. (New York: Barnes and Noble Books, 1970.)
Kermode has a fine introduction to the play (as well as fuller textual commentary than the Pelican edition) that includes discussion of the text, date, and themes of the play, together with background material on "the new world," art and nature, pastoral tragicomedy, and a brief review of criticism (now out-of-date).

McFarland, Thomas. "So Rare a Wondered Father: *The Tempest* and the Vision of Paradise." In *Shakespeare's Pastoral Comedy,* pp. 146–75. Chapel Hill: University of North Carolina Press, 1972. And Marsh, Derrick R. "*The Tempest.*" In *The Recurring Miracle,* pp. 162–91. Lincoln: University of Nebraska Press, 1962, reprinted 1969.
Because of their opposite views of Prospero, I recommend reading both essays, allowing each to balance the other. McFarland equates Prospero with God, whereas Marsh finds him to be a failed human being, due to "a fundamental flaw" in his philosophy; that is, "he sees life as split into the mutually opposing elements of the spiritual and the physical, when really they are indivisible." Each essay contains worthwhile material for the student of *The Tempest,* but each is clearly dominated by a determined view of Prospero either as a god or as a negativistic and world-weary man.

Rickey, Mary Ellen. "Prospero's Living Drolleries." In *Renaissance Papers 1964,* pp. 35–42. Edited by S. K. Heninger, Jr., Peter G. Philias, and George Walton Williams. Rutland, Vermont: Charles E. Tuttle Co., for the Southeastern Renaissance Conference, 1965.
Rickey examines what she considers to be Christian données for three of the play's actions: the chess game, the magic banquet, and the Dantesque punishment of the low comics (Stephano, Trinculo, and Caliban).

Summers, Joseph H. "The Anger of Prospero." *Michigan Quarterly Review* 12 (1973):116–35.

Summers finds that Prospero, "with the possible exception of Lear, shows the shortest temper of any admirable character in Shakespeare." Although Prospero's anger differs from that of the villains, it is one of the characteristics that "bind[s] him to humanity both on the island and in the audience." Through his control of the play's actions, not only are the other characters purged to some extent of their flaws, but Prospero also is purged of his anger, finding the rarer action to be in forgiveness rather than vengeance.

Notes

1. For a fuller discussion of this scene, see Joan Hartwig, *Shakespeare's Tragicomic Vision* (Baton Rouge: Louisiana State University Press, 1972), pp. 142–49.
2. For further definition, see my essay, "Cloten, Autolycus, and Caliban: Bearers of Parodic Burdens," in *Shakespeare's Romances Reconsidered,* ed. Carol McGinnis Kay and Henry E. Jacobs (Lincoln and London: University of Nebraska Press, 1978), pp. 93–94.
3. Allan H. Gilbert makes a similar point in "*The Tempest:* Parallelism in Characters and Situations," *Journal of English and Germanic Philology* 14 (1915):73.
4. For an elaboration of these ideas, see *Shakespeare's Tragicomic Vision,* pp. 162–64.
5. Robert Ralston Cawley makes interesting correlations between verbal echoes and attitudes expressed in the play and contemporary travel literature in "Shakespeare's Use of the Voyagers in *The Tempest,*" *PMLA,* 41 (1926):688–726. See especially pp. 720–21 about the common practice of carrying Indians from the New World back to London in order to display them for money.
6. Peter J. Seng has commentary on the text, music, and dramatic function of all the songs in the play in *The Vocal Songs in the Plays of Shakespeare: A Critical History* (Cambridge, Mass.: Harvard University Press, 1967), pp. 248–72.
7. Harry Epstein discusses Prospero's trial in detail, especially "the temptation of his magic" in "The Divine Comedy of *The Tempest,*" *Shakespeare Studies,* 8 (1975):279–96.
8. For fuller discussion of the effects of the Epilogue, see *Shakespeare's Tragicomic Vision,* pp. 20–22 and 170–74.

SELF-TEST

Multiple-choice Questions
1. What is similar about the way that Caliban and Miranda react when they each encounter men whom they've never seen before?
    a. Both are shocked at how puny the man seems.
    b. Both suspect that they are under a magic spell that makes them see strange creature(s).
    c. Both see something divine about the strange creature(s).
    d. Both see something evil about the strange creature(s).
    e. Both let out cries for help.
2. Which of the following represents a parallel between Caliban and Ferdinand?
    a. Both are devastatingly ugly.
    b. Both are, by their natures, slaves.
    c. Both are made to perform menial, slavelike labor.
    d. Neither lusts for Miranda.
    e.. Neither accepts his condition of slavery.
3. Which of the following best describes the difference between Prospero the magician and Prospero the man?
    a. Prospero the magician is cold and distant; Prospero the man is warm and tender.
    b. Prospero the magician is strong and aggressive; Prospero the man is weak and passive.
    c. Prospero the magician is an omnipotent master; Prospero the man is uninformed and unwise.
    d. Prospero the magician displays a wealth of emotions and attitudes; Prospero the man is very limited in his range of reactions.
    e. Prospero the magician is calculating and in control; Prospero the man displays a full range of human emotions, weaknesses, and strengths.
4. Match each of the characters in Column I with the appropriate incident of parody or parallel action in Column II.

Column I	Column II
_____ a. Miranda/Caliban	1. accused of attempting to steal the island
_____ b. Ferdinand/Caliban	2. raised swords and impotence
_____ c. Prospero/Ferdinand	3. ignorance of outside world and an innocent reaction to it
_____ d. Stephano/Sebastian	4. sexual desire for Miranda
_____ e. Ferdinand/Sebastian	5. contemplation of regicide

5. Which of the following is the best example of how Shakespeare shifts the audience's perspective and integrates the audience into the play's action?
    a. allowing the audience to believe the storm wracking the ship was real, then revealing that it was contrived by magic
    b. allowing the audience to believe that Caliban is a "noble savage," then exposing him as a real savage
    c. allowing the audience to believe Ferdinand has been drowned, then revealing he is safe

d. encouraging the audience to despise Antonio, the usurper Duke of Milan, then showing that he has many admirable traits
e. leading the audience to believe Prospero will use his magic to get revenge, then showing him forgiving those who abused him

6. Match each of the characters in Column I with the trial he or she must undergo in Column II.

    Column I
    _____ a. Ariel
    _____ b. Ferdinand
    _____ c. Prospero
    _____ d. Alonso
    _____ e. Caliban
    _____ f. Stephano/Trinculo

    Column II
    1. suffering in the belief that he has lost a son
    2. suffering servitude as a test of virtue and honest intentions
    3. suffering the disillusionment with a newly found "god"
    4. suffering servitude as a repayment of a debt of freedom
    5. suffering loss of control and final acceptance of human limitations
    6. suffering physical torment for physical indulgences

7. What is similar about the way that Ferdinand and Stephano *first* react to the island's inhabitants?
    a. Both are frightened.
    b. Both are astonished that the inhabitants speak their language.
    c. Both are curious as to how the inhabitants came to be on the island.
    d. Both draw their swords to defend themselves from the strange creature.
    e. Both suspect they are under some magic spell.

8. Which of the following is a central theme in the masque that Prospero presents to celebrate the betrothal of his daughter and Ferdinand?
    a. the necessity of securing the approval of the gods before acting
    b. the danger of lust marring the union of lovers
    c. the importance of love in a marriage
    d. the realization that nothing, not even love, lasts forever
    e. the importance of forgiving even the worst offender

9. Which of the following is *not* a device used in *The Tempest* to integrate the audience into the play's action?
    a. use of the familiar "love at first sight" in an unfamiliar setting
    b. Prospero's final act of turning over power to the audience
    c. presenting a character invisible to other characters, but visible to the audience
    d. establishing an empathetic bond between the audience and Caliban
    e. dislocating the audience's perception of reality as well as the characters from the ship

10. Which best describes the personality of Caliban?
    a. noble savage
    b. beast with a heart of gold
    c. debauched, born slave
    d. ignorant, yet wise
    e. perceptive judge of character

Short-answer Essay Questions
1. Some of the occurrences in the play obviously are the result of Prospero's magic, such as the banquet (III, iii), the masque (IV, i), the spells that freeze characters in their tracks (I, ii, 467; III, iii, 67–68). What are some of the events that seem to happen naturally (that is, without the operation of magical charms) that become magical, either by the way in which they are presented or in retrospect?
2. What function do the courtiers Francisco and Adrian serve?
3. For which characters does Caliban offer the clearest parody?
4. How is the audience made to feel a part of the ongoing action of the play? How is our perception of reality dislocated?
5. What is Prospero's "rarer action" and how do we know it is difficult for him?

Questions for Reflection
1. Consider the frequent occurrence of music and song in the play. Does this pervasive musical quality add anything to the play's magic?
2. What would Prospero be without his magic powers? What sort of father and ruler do we see him to be with his magic and without his magic? How do you explain his initial hostility toward Ferdinand?
3. There are definite "fairy-tale" elements in the play. Do these make it a piece of escapist literature? If not, consider what Shakespeare does to "ground" his fantasy story in reality. Are there people and situations with which we can identify or sympathize or both?
4. What is the best way to describe Ariel? Why is he so important to Prospero and to the play's effect?
5. This play has more original stage directions than most of Shakespeare's other plays. It is also more compact, observing the classical unities of time, place, and action; and it is probably the last play he wrote for his London repertory company before retiring to Stratford. Do these facts lead you to any conclusions about Shakespeare's attitude toward this particular play?

ANSWER KEY

Answers to Multiple-choice Questions
1. c (essay; I, ii; II, ii)
2. c (essay; I, ii; III, i)
3. e (essay; evidence throughout the play)
4. a: 3 (essay; I, ii)
   b: 4 (essay; I, ii)
   c: 1 (essay; I, ii)
   d: 5 (essay; II, i; II, ii)
   e: 2 (essay; II, i; III, iii)
5. a (essay; I, i–I, ii)
6. a: 4 (essay; I, ii and throughout the play)
   b: 2 (essay; I, ii; III, i)
   c: 5 (essay; V, i)
   d: 1 (essay; II, i)
   e: 3 (essay; V, i)
   f: 6 (essay; IV, i)

7. b (essay; II, i; III, ii)
8. b (essay; IV, i)
9. d (essay; evidence throughout the play)
10. c (essay; evidence throughout the play)

Suggested Answers to Short-answer Essay Questions

1. Miranda's sleep in II, i; Miranda and Ferdinand's falling in love as staged by Prospero; Miranda and Ferdinand's being discovered at chess, which Sebastian calls a "most high miracle"; Caliban's dream speech (III, ii, 132–40); Caliban's conversion at the end; Prospero's forgiveness of Antonio; the reconciliation of the entire group—to Miranda and Caliban the assembled court group seems a magical vision; the Epilogue that brings the audience into the play's province in almost a magical way.

2. Francisco and Adrian have very little to say, although they are given a line here and there. They may have been intended for larger characterization that Shakespeare discarded after he got into the play. As they stand, however, they do little more than enlarge the visual numbers of the court group and act as a benign counterpart to Sebastian and Antonio. They are also part of that assemblage at the end of the play that causes such wonder in Miranda and Caliban.

3. For Ferdinand, lust and servitude, and praise of Miranda's beauty; for Miranda, innocence and awe of strangers; for Ariel, who is like air, Caliban presents an earthbound figure; for Prospero, he parodies the notion of ruling the island; for Antonio, he is a would-be murderer/usurper.

4. We are dislocated initially by the differing views of what the tempest was. We are drawn in at various times by the familiar (such as love at first sight) in the midst of the unfamiliar. But most of all we are drawn into the play by Prospero's Epilogue, which grants us the power and privilege of magician and playwright, both of whom are under our control.

5. Prospero's "rarer action is/ In virtue than in vengeance" (V, i, 27–28), and is to forgive the injustices done to him when he was formerly Duke of Milan. It is especially difficult to forgive Antonio, who indicates no change from his former villainy. It is likewise difficult for Prospero to include Caliban in his harmonious reconciliation, since he thinks that Caliban likewise is incapable of reclamation. He indicates his perturbation after the masque and in the final scene: "my beating mind" (IV, i, 163) and "this thing of darkness" (V, i, 275) speeches.